1998

W9-CLF-756

Being Responsive
to Cultural
Differences

SPONSORED BY THE
**AMERICAN ASSOCIATION of COLLEGES
for TEACHER EDUCATION**

Being Responsive to Cultural Differences

How Teachers Learn

Editor:
Mary E. Dilworth

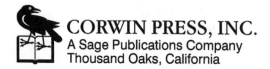

CORWIN PRESS, INC.
A Sage Publications Company
Thousand Oaks, California

For information:

Corwin Press, Inc.
A Sage Publications Company
2455 Teller Road
Thousand Oaks, California 91320
E-mail: order@corwin.sagepub.com

SAGE Publications Ltd.
6 Bonhill Street
London EC2A 4PU
United Kingdom

SAGE Publications India Pvt. Ltd.
M-32 Market
Greater Kailash I
New Delhi 110 048 India

Printed in the United States of America

Library of Congress Cataloging-in-Publication Data

Being responsive to cultural differences: How teachers learn /
    Mary E. Dilworth, editor.
        p. cm.
    Includes bibliographical references and index.
    ISBN 0-8039-6669-5 (cloth: acid-free paper). —
    ISBN 0-8039-6670-9 (pbk.: acid-free paper)
    1. Teachers—Training of—Social aspects—United States.
    2. Multicultural education—United States. 3. Minorities—
    Education—United States. I. Dilworth, Mary E. (Mary Elizabeth),
    1950- .
LB1715.B42 1998
370.117—dc21   97-21133

This book is printed on acid-free paper.

98 99 00 01 02 10 9 8 7 6 5 4 3 2 1

Production Editor: Sanford Robinson
Production Assistant: Lynn Miyata
Editorial Assistant: Kristen L. Gibson
Typesetter/Designer: Janelle LeMaster
Cover Designer: Marcia M. Rosenburg
Print Buyer: Anna Chin

Contents

PART II

PART III

Preface

Culturally responsive teaching practice shows promise in improving academic achievement among students from low income and disenfranchised racial-ethnic and linguistic minority groups. The research is ripe with information that explains the importance of embracing a broader conception of what is good and appropriate in culturally responsive teaching. At the same time, teacher educators and students thirst for rich descriptions and examples of how these new understandings look and feel. This volume is intended to contribute to this dimension.

It is unique in the abundance of new voices that build on the notions of established contemporary educators. In addition, the authors rely, more so than others, on knowledge gained directly from practice. The readings are organized in three parts. Part I focuses on the perceptions and senses of those grappling with culturally responsive practice. Part II suggests ways in which attention to culture can influence the manner in which we approach instruction, and Part III, varying approaches to teacher education practice.

Part I begins with "The Presence of an Absence: Issues of Race in Teacher Education at a Predominantly White College Campus" by Pearl M. Rosenberg. In this chapter, Rosenberg skillfully presents a picture of the challenges and dilemmas of majority teachers striving to be culturally responsive in their practice. Jane Agee provides a case study that suggests that preservice teachers of color may find ideology and hierarchy of power in a school culture very difficult to negotiate without a specific network of mentoring, in "Confronting Issues of Race and Power in the Culture of Schools: A Case Study of a Preservice Teacher." Teachers' confidence in their abilities to teach youngsters essential knowledge and skills is addressed by Valerie Ooka Pang and

Velma A. Sablan in "Teacher Efficacy: How Do Teachers Feel About Their Abilities to Teach African American Students?" The authors find that negative feelings about teacher abilities to address the needs of African American students emerge from negative feelings about African American parents. They further conclude that preservice teachers demonstrate higher levels of efficacy than inservice teachers.

In Part II, Michael Webb's "Culture: A View Toward the Unexplored Frontier" provides poignant examples as he argues for cultural considerations in curriculum, expectations, learning styles, and professional development. In "The African Advantage: Using African Culture to Enhance Culturally Responsive Comprehensive Teacher Education," Mwangaza Michael-Bandele posits that within the African cultural context are conceptual frameworks valuable to teaching and learning. Using various African proverbs, she allows the reader to explore the value of African cultural contexts to the development of multicultural teacher education strategies.

In "Multicultural Content Infusion by Student Teachers: Perceptions and Beliefs of Cooperating Teachers," Michael Vavrus and Mustafa Ozcan examine cooperating teachers' notions and perceptions of multicultural content infusion by student teachers. In doing so, they also contribute to a greater understanding of cooperating teachers themselves.

In "Prospective Teachers Constructing Their Own Knowledge in Multicultural Education," Sharon Adelman Reyes, Nayda Capella-Santana, and Lena Licón Khisty offer a rich description of a course in multicultural education for prospective teachers that was designed around the participants' construction of their own knowledge. The authors provide their informal writings, which indicate that this approach affects cognitive processes and internalization.

Part III begins with "Culturally Literate Teachers: Preparation for 21st Century Schools." Claudette Merrell Ligons, Luis A. Rosado, and W. Robert Houston provide a useful conceptual framework and explicitly detail strategies for culturally responsive practice. In "What Difference Does Diversity Make? Educating Preservice Teachers for Learner Diversity," Andrea Guillaume, Carmen Zuniga, and Ivy Yee offer their findings in a study of an intensive preservice preparation course for cultural responsiveness. The authors make a number of useful observations regarding the effects of certain methods (e.g., case studies). They also conclude that moving prospective teachers toward thoughtful, integrated treatment of diversity issues present difficulties and dilemmas. "Pursuing the Possibilities of Passion: The Affective Domain of Multicultural Education," by Francisco A. Rios, Janet E. McDaniel, and Laura P. Stowell, show how the context of community, university, program, and course in multicultural education worked to shift prospective teachers' attitudes and beliefs.

In "Multicultural Education in Practice: What Do Teachers Say?," Constance L. Walker and Diane J. Tedick examine practicing teachers' descriptions of the manifestations of diversity in classroom settings. Last, Mary E. Dilworth provides thoughts on the "Old Messages With New Meanings" that the volume offers.

About the Authors

Jane Agee, PhD, is Assistant Professor of Language in Education at the State University of New York at Albany. Her research interests include teacher education and teaching literature in secondary schools. For her recent publications on teacher education, see *English Education, Signal Journal,* and *The Journal of Literacy Research* (in press).

Nayda Capella-Santana received her PhD from the University of Illinois at Chicago. She is the Dual Language Coordinator at Sabin Magnet School in Chicago. Her research interests include multicultural and bilingual education, teacher education, and parental involvement in curriculum. She is the author of "Parents: A Source of Knowledge," *IATE Newsletter, 44*; and "Developing Culturally Relevant Curriculum: Parents as a Source of Knowledge," *Critical Issues in Teacher Education.*

Mary E. Dilworth is Senior Director for Research for the American Association of Colleges for Teacher Education and Director of the ERIC Clearinghouse on Teaching and Teacher Education. She received her EdD in Higher Education Administration from the Catholic University of America. She has served on a number of national education advisory boards, is a member of Phi Delta Kappa, and has written numerous articles and reports. Widely recognized and honored for her contributions to teaching and teacher education, she is listed in *Who's Who Among Black Americans, Who's Who in the East,* and the *World Who's Who of Women.*

Andrea Guillaume is Associate Professor in the Department of Elementary and Bilingual Education at California State University, Fullerton. She earned her PhD at the University of California, Riverside. Her recent publications are found in *Action in Teacher Education, Teacher Education Quarterly,* and *Teaching and Teacher Education.* Her particular research interest is teacher cognition.

W. Robert Houston is Professor and Executive Director of the Institute for Urban Education at the University of Houston. He earned the EdD degree from the University of Texas-Austin. His research interests include teacher education and university-school partnerships. His most recent books are *Handbook of Research on Teacher Education* and *Encouraging Reflective Practice in Education.*

Lena Licón Khisty is Associate Professor of Curriculum and Instruction at the University of Illinois, Chicago. Her research focuses on issues of discourse, pedagogical practices, professional development, and systemic change related to academic involvement, particularly among Latinos in mathematics. Her coauthored chapter "Challenging Conventional Wisdom: A Case Study" is to appear in the forthcoming book *Changing the Faces of Mathematics: Perspectives on Latinos and Latinas.*

Claudette Merrell Ligons is Professor and Chair of the Department of Curriculum and Instruction, College of Education, Texas Southern University. She earned her EdD degree in Multicultural and Competency-Based Education from the University of Houston. Her research interests include equity issues in education and school variables that foster student success. Recent publications focus on student success in urban schools and strategies for enhancing student performance in the early school years.

Janet E. McDaniel, PhD, is Associate Professor at California State University–San Marcos, where she serves as Coordinator of Middle Level Teacher Education. Her research interests are middle school teaching and teacher education. Her recent coauthored book is *Working with Middle School Students* (Stowell, Rios, McDaniel, & Christopher, 1996).

Mwangaza Michael-Bandele is Research Associate at the American Association of Colleges for Teacher Education and Adjunct Lecturer in African and African American History at Bowie State University. At AACTE, she has coordinated national demonstration projects as well as video and teleconference production. Designing and implementing empowerment seminars for teachers is her passion. She is currently a doctoral student in African diaspora history at Morgan State University.

Mustafa Ozcan earned his PhD from the University of Iowa in Sociology of Education. Currently, he is Assistant Professor at Clarke College (IA) and teaches courses in multicultural education. His research interests include the influence of social class, culture, race, and gender on student and teacher behavior.

Valerie Ooka Pang is Professor in the School of Teacher Education at San Diego State University. Widely published in journals such as *Harvard Educational Review, Phi Delta Kappan,* and *Equity and Excellence,* her work focuses on teacher education, multicultural education, and Asian Pacific American children. Recipient of the 1997 Distinguished Scholars Award from the American Educational Research Association's Committee on the Role and Status of Minorities in Education, she has served as consultant and staff developer to a wide range of organizations such as *Sesame Street* and Fox Children's Network.

Sharon Adelman Reyes is a doctoral candidate in curriculum design at the University of Illinois at Chicago. Her dissertation topic focuses on Spanish second-language acquisition in young children and related issues of culture and meaning. Other research interests include bilingual, multicultural, and arts education.

Francisco A. Rios, PhD, is Associate Professor in the College of Education at California State University-San Marcos (CSUSM). His academic interests focus on teaching and learning, cognitive science applied to education, the Latino experience in education, and multicultural-multilingual education. His teaching specialties include learning and instruction and multicultural education.

Luis A. Rosado, Associate Professor, is Director of Field Services and Certification at Texas Southern University, Houston, Texas. He holds an EdD degree in Bilingual Education from Texas A&M University in Kingsville, Texas. His research interests are cross-cultural communication, bilingual education, and teacher education. He has published in the areas of parental involvement and Spanish linguistics.

Pearl M. Rosenberg is Assistant Professor of Education at Cedar Crest College, PA, teaching courses in educational psychology, teacher education, and women's studies and is Director of the Academic Resource Center. Previously a member of the teacher education faculty at the University of New Hampshire, her research interests include women and education and the social and psychological development of teachers. She is published in Fine, Weis, Powell, and Wong's (1997) *Off White: Readings on Race, Power, and Society.*

Velma A. Sablan is Associate Professor in the Division of Foundations, Educational Research, and Human Services at the College of Education, University of Guam. She also serves as Core Faculty for Research and Dissemination for the Guam University Affiliated Programs and is Chair of the UOG Faculty Council. Her dissertation, *Teacher Efficacy in the Pacific Island of Guam,* is scheduled to be published next year.

Laura P. Stowell, PhD, is Associate Professor in the College of Education at California State University-San Marcos. Her responsibilities include teaching courses in language and literacy at the elementary and middle school levels and children's literacy at the elementary and middle school levels as well as children's literature. She was chosen Outstanding Professor of the Year, 1996-1997 at CSUSM.

Diane J. Tedick is Associate Professor in Second Languages and Cultures Education in the College of Education and Human Development at the University of Minnesota, Twin Cities. She earned her PhD at the Ohio State University, Columbus. She prepares teachers for ESL, immersion, and foreign language classrooms, and her research interests include teacher preparation, second language literacy, and content-based language instruction. Her recent publications appear in *Teaching Education, Modern Language Journal, Foreign Language Annals,* the 1996 Northeast Conference Reports, *Foreign Languages for All: Challenges and Choices,* and a forthcoming volume, *Content-Based Instruction in Foreign Language Education: Models and Methods.*

Michael Vavrus is Director of the Master in Teaching Program at The Evergreen State College in Olympia, Washington, and is past president of the Association of Independent Colleges for Teacher Education. *Education Studies* has recently published his essay reviews on Native American education, historical dimensions of multicultural education, and teacher education. He holds a PhD from Michigan State University.

Constance L. Walker is Associate Professor in Second Languages and Cultures Education in the College of Education and Human Development at the University of Minnesota, Twin Cities. She earned her PhD at the University of Illinois, Urbana-Champaign. She works in the preparation of teachers for ESL, bilingual, and foreign language settings, and her research interests lie in minority student achievement, multicultural education, and the preparation of teachers for diverse student populations. Her recent publications appear in the *Journal of Teacher Education, Modern Language Journal, Foreign Language Annals,* and the 1996 Northeast Conference Reports, *Foreign Languages for All: Challenges and Choices.*

Michael Webb is currently a program officer in New Visions for Public Schools in New York City. He has worked in urban education for nearly 25 years, as a teacher, researcher, administrator, and policy analyst. For three years, he led national initiatives to increase the role of parents and families in mathematics and science education reform. He also worked in universities in Nigeria and Egypt. In 1989, he founded the International Youth Leadership Institute, which sponsors youth development and overseas study programs for high school students. He has published numerous monographs and authored major reports commissioned by the National Educational Goals Panel, Commission on Students of African Descent of the New York City Board of Education, State University of New York African American Institute, and others. His articles have appeared in *Equity and Choice, PTA Today, State of Black America,* and *Business Monthly.* He has also contributed to several textbooks on African American history. He has received academic degrees from St. John Fisher College, San Francisco State University, and Teachers College, Columbia University.

Ivy Yee is Assistant Professor in the Department of Elementary and Bilingual Education at California State University, Fullerton. She earned her PhD at the University of California, Los Angeles. Her most recent article appeared in the *Journal of Research and Development in Education.* Her research interests include multicultural education and teacher preparation.

Carmen Zuniga is Associate Professor in the Department of Elementary and Bilingual Education at California State University, Fullerton. She earned her PhD at the University of Illinois, Champaign. Her recent publications are found in the *Journal of Educational Issues of Language Minority Students, Journal of Teacher Education,* and *Teacher Education Quarterly.* Her research interests include teacher preparation for diversity and language and literacy development.

PART I

The Presence of an Absence

Issues of Race in Teacher Education at a
Predominantly White College Campus

■ *Pearl M. Rosenberg*

> *Why do we need to think about black people when black people aren't around?*

A white preservice education student wrote this question on an anonymous course evaluation for an educational psychology course that I
teach at a northern New England college campus. Based on my observations of the students I have worked with in this predominantly white
teacher education program in the past 4 years, I believe that this stu-

AUTHOR'S NOTE: A shorter version of this chapter was presented at the April
1993 meeting of the American Educational Research Association in Atlanta, GA.
Early thinking about these issues resulted from many conversations with Marilyn Cochran-Smith and Michelle Fine. In addition, I am indebted to Cindy Cohen, Ann Diller, Barbara Houston, Dana Kaminstein, Donna Qualley, and Paula
Salvio for their friendship and collegiality around the sharing of ideas and the
editing of this manuscript. And I am grateful for the many students who allow
me to document their experience of becoming a teacher.

dent's question is indicative of the thinking of many other students, who communicate a similar curiosity through their writing and speaking, although perhaps not spoken as boldly as this anonymous student.

Most students I have taught in this program appear respectful of the need for intercultural sensitivity as it pertains to educators who may work in culturally diverse settings. At the same time, unobtrusive measures, such as anonymous course evaluations, highlight student ambivalence as to why these conversations need to take place in environments where the representation of people who are different from them in race, culture, and ethnicity is very low.

The necessity of preparing all preservice teachers to work with culturally diverse students in culturally diverse settings should be clear. The racial composition of the group entering the teaching force is overwhelmingly white, with African Americans, Asian Americans, Latinos, and Native Americans together representing less than 10% of prospective teachers and steadily declining (Cochran-Smith, 1995). What may be less clear is how our experience as white teacher educators and preservice teachers stems for most of us from dominant whiteness in classrooms, workplaces, and communities.

Drawing on the data of student responses to the course curriculum and their views of pedagogy implicit in their papers, journal entries, group projects and presentations, and course evaluations, I have begun to analyze the nature of my students' responses to what it means to address issues of race in teacher education at a predominantly white college campus.

As I try to bring issues of race and racism to consciousness in my students, I view race as a set of social relations that are socially and historically constructed and subject to political tensions and contradictions (Hall, 1992). Thus, race is not taken as a stable category. This is fitting, because my work with preservice teachers on these issues is often filled with conjecture and detours. I believe this is so for two reasons: (a) the nature of this work is self-reflexive, for my thoughts, feelings, and understandings of race and racism are changing as well as my students— but more significant is (b) the challenge of having conversations with students in what I have called "the presence of an absence," which places us all for the most part in the position of having to imagine other people's lives refracted through the various lenses of the news and entertainment media.

I am concerned here with the primary tension I have discovered in trying to help preservice teachers in a predominantly white teacher education program to consider race as a factor in preparing to teach in our culture. For many white students, thinking about race becomes a highly charged emotional experience resulting in resistance, misunderstanding, rage, and feelings of inefficacy (Tatum, 1992, 1994). To "unleash the unpopular" (Britzman, 1991) calls into question what for many is already settled. In this case, what is already settled is how students think of themselves as white, if they think about it at all. Although emotional responses to the issue of race should be viewed as a potential source of energy for learning about a multicultural society, too often I see in my students feelings of empathy for and identification with groups not present. These feelings may be in response to the helplessness that they often feel when learning about race, racism, and teaching, or the genuine desire to know or understand the other. Nevertheless, the tolerance of many white students for learning about those different from themselves in race, culture, and ethnicity appears to be dependent on the extent to which they can reconstruct those others in the image of themselves. It is important that we check this impulse in ourselves as white teacher educators and our students who want to be teachers, especially when those who are different from us in race, culture, and ethnicity are not immediately present.

■ The Presence of an Absence

The "presence of an absence" as I am defining it here has to do with the figurative presence of race and racism, even in the virtual absence of those groups against which racism is most directed. As of this writing, out of a student population of 12, 500 students at this university (including both undergraduate and graduate students), there are 183 persons identified as Asian American, 117 persons identified as Latino, 90 persons identified as African American, and 12 student identified as Native American. The presence of these students in the Education Department in particular is limited to 4 African Americans and 2 Asian American students out of a group of 405 master's degree students.

There are many serious, well-planned attempts by faculty and administration to attract more students of different racial and cultural identities to the university and to address racism on this campus; however, conservative forces are strong in this state where most of the enrolled students have spent their whole lives.

There are examples of both overt forms of racism and general discomfort and tension around issues of race in the college community, as evidenced by visual artifacts and public conversations. Most of the examples of this discomfort that I have observed in the community over the past few years are aimed at the black population in particular. I have found pamphlets on the wall in a local post office from the Grand Wizard of the Klu Klux Klan asking for membership. Racial slurs are scrawled on walls of dorms, especially after programs on campus celebrating black experience. And conversations fraught with racist undertones take place periodically (especially in January) about why Martin Luther King's birthday should not be a legal holiday in New Hampshire, the only state in the union not to so recognize it.[1]

In my educational psychology class (a foundations course required for all preservice teachers in the master's program), we spend considerable time looking at various ways in which the ideology of equality of opportunity and access obscures the actual unequal distribution of resources and outcomes for a variety of individuals based on social class, gender, and race. Students are asked to read and write and think about classicism, sexism, and racism as systems of advantage based on class, gender, and race. In short, they are asked to know the "other" not as a category of person but as a process of domination. This is the backdrop for looking at classical topics in educational psychology (e.g., testing, motivation, cognitive, and social development).

Race comes up in this class in one of three ways: (a) I have assigned readings or I have asked the students to engage in a variety of workshop activities that address issues of race in education. Students may be asked to respond to readings or activities in the form of informal writings, class discussion, or both; (b) students may choose to write about race as one of many topics throughout the term for required papers; or (c) students may not purposely choose to address issues of race, but in the course of working on another issue, it comes up for them (as in the example to follow).

The following scenario characterizes the preservice teachers I work with in teacher education and helps to illuminate my primary concern in this chapter.

In the Spring of 1992, the LA riots were flaring in response to the courtroom decision surrounding the beating of motorist Rodney King by some members of the Los Angeles police department. In my educational psychology class (that term, an all-white class except for one Asian American male), a group of students were showing a clip from the film *Boyz N' the Hood* as part of their class presentation on stress and adolescence. The student group announced that their choice of this film was based on their collective opinion that this film portrayed adolescent life in an honest way. There was no mention of the fact that the story took place in a black community in general, or that it dealt with gang violence in particular.

Boyz N' the Hood involves a young male protagonist named Trey, a sensitive, promising teenager, who is portrayed in relation to his father, friends, and community as engaged in a towering struggle of how to become a black man with integrity in racist America. The segment that the student group shared with the class on this day shows the teenager driving home one night as he is pulled over by a cop and harassed for apparently no other reason than his race. Ironically, the cop was black as well. The young man returns to his girlfriend's house in great emotional pain; the harassment has catalyzed the daily pain and torment that he lives with and tries so hard to rise above. He writhes and screams in the doorway inside of his girlfriend's house, heavy metal bars across the door frame the background of the scene of the young man who ultimately collapses into his girlfriend's arms, sobbing inconsolably.

The class watched this episode respectfully and listened to the presentation that followed. Most students seemed to appreciate the group's presentation as evidenced by their thoughtful questions and comments throughout. Student responses dealt primarily with points about how adolescents feel powerless in their daily lives in general and admissions about how teen boys are often harassed undeservingly by police officers in particular. Because these presentations are designed purposely by me for students to be in charge of class time and discussion, I remained silent.

Finally, the one Asian American student in the class, David, directed the class's attention to the fact that these characters are black and expressed his concern about the class not viewing it in that context. One student in the class, Jennifer, had begun to cry while watching the film clip. It seemed that David's honest observation of the class has empowered Jennifer to speak directly about her feelings. Jennifer expressed her sadness about the LA riots and now having seen this character on film in such torment, expressed great empathy for his pain. She was fervent in her declaration that no person should be treated this way and said she has been feeling "very bad" about the King verdict. She added that although she felt bad, she did not know what to do about it [racism].

■ White Racial Identity Development

Beverly Tatum claims that emotional responses students have to hearing about race and racism are quite predictable and often related to one's own racial identity development (Tatum, 1992). She refers to the six stages of white students' racial identity development articulated by Helms (1990) as ranging from an early stage of development (the Contact stage), which is characterized by a lack of awareness of cultural and institutional racism, and evolving more toward not just awareness of the issues of race and how it affects others in general but a growing sense of oneself as white in relation to other groups of color as well (Helms, 1990). Tatum points out that individuals who continue to have limited interaction with people of color, or exposure to information about race and racism, may remain at the Contact stage "indefinitely." The new understanding that may result from contact with persons or information marks the beginning of the Disintegration stage. Tatum explains that at this stage, "the bliss of ignorance or lack of awareness is replaced by the discomfort of guilt, shame, and sometimes anger at the recognition of one's own advantage because of being White and the acknowledgement of the role of Whites in the maintenance of a racist system" (Tatum, 1992, p. 13). Tatum, who is an African American, works with predominantly white students in Holyoke, Massachusetts. Her situation is different from a white teacher teaching whites, for her presence offers her white students an opportunity to engage directly in a relationship with her as an African American in a way that I cannot.

I would characterize the students in the teacher education program that I work with as being, for the most part, caring individuals who because of their lack of contact with diverse groups have formed their opinions and behaviors about people of color around imagined circumstances. They often speak with great feeling for these groups with whom they have had little contact. But their feelings cannot mask their lack of awareness of the cultural and institutional racism that oppresses these groups, issues that rarely are recognized in the expression of their concern for these groups.

Thus, when students express their care for others who are not present, their expressions often sound naive because they do not have access or experience themselves in relation to the other. They may be experiencing an involvement with the other or desire for the other's well-being but are unable to truly envision themselves in the other's shoes.

Nel Noddings (1984) differentiates between *caring for* and *caring about*. She notes that caring *for* is a relation and a relation one can have only with those who are proximate to oneself. Thus, on this analysis, the students who address racism in the presence of an absence can care about others as opposed to caring for them.

This circumstance of dealing with issues of race and racism in this way suggests to me that when white people say we care about those groups or individuals that we are not in relation to, it can sometimes be a way of actually gaining privilege over the very individuals we claim to care about. For we must assume that the other wants to be in relation to us, or even worse, that we may know what the other wants without even being told. Moreover, this unidirectional analysis of one-way caring reinforces oppressive institutions, the very political circumstance that is crucial to unpack with preservice teachers. So instead of developing a critique of the institutional realities they will be participating in, they will find themselves in the position of caretaker instead.

The students who were processing their reactions to the clip from *Boyz N' the Hood* were identifying with the main character Trey's frustration and rage about feeling powerless against forces about which they have little control. But there is a fine line between these young white males feeling similar to Trey without co-opting the significant differences that his oppression as a young black male creates.

The pedagogical question, it seems to me, is how to build on this emotional recognition of sameness toward an intellectual understanding or critique of differences.

■ The Politics of Empathy

Jennifer, the student in the classroom scenario who expressed her feelings, was acknowledging the pain of the character in the film and making a connection with the others who may be suffering because of racism in our country. Although one would not want to deny the progress that this student and others like her may make along these lines by expressing their feelings about race and racism, I believe that this scenario should be told as a cautionary tale.

Those of us who teach in conservative environments could view this student as exhibiting strength of character in this predominantly white classroom by naming an injustice, raising important questions for the class about individual responsibility around racism, and expressing true empathy for other people. Her behavior may be considered noteworthy and admirable. However, even though empathy is an admirable trait and a needed first step in the education of our students around issues of racism, teaching for empathy is not enough. Empathy has its own dangers. It can, I think, create a false sense of involvement.

I am defining *empathy* as identification with and understanding of another's situation, feelings, motives. It is the aspect of "identification" and how it is used by my students that concerns me the most, especially if we consider how the process of identification may be used to assuage one's own sadness or guilt.

I see a desire for identification in my students who are eager to explore their own biographies around issues of growth and development in my educational psychology class. Unfortunately, these students often use other people's oppression in the identification and interpretation of their own lives. In my class, we read classic articles by Rist (1970) on teacher expectations and the self-fulfilling prophecy in ghetto education, Gilmore (1985) on inner-city girls creating their own expressions of literacy using jump-rope rhymes in response to the rules of the school, and Fine (1985) on why students stay in and drop out of school in the urban ghetto. Many students respond to these readings in class by exclaiming, "Oh, I know exactly what he [or she] means! The same thing happened to me [in the mountains of New Hampshire]." They often see these narratives, theirs and the young people in these inner-city ghettos, as the same. I believe that it is crucial for these students not to weave their narratives together with their inner-city counterparts in a blanket of shared victimization that obscures the ways that racist domination affects the lives of marginalized groups in our society.

Megan Boler (1994) warns us of the "risks of empathy" and claims that using the model of "social imagination" to help our white students imagine themselves in the "others'" shoes can allow the [student] to indulge in nothing more than a "harmonious experience of reversibility and the pleasure of identification," but at the expense of what?

No matter how genuine and heartfelt our feelings of brotherhood and sisterhood may be, our caring is made problematic by what Ron Scaap (hooks, 1992) describes as the "politics of empathy." Scaap claims that those who care (liberals) may think they have a vision of diversity and plurality while clinging to notions of sameness where we are all one. He notes,

> Liberals may pride themselves in their ability to tolerate others, but it is only after the other has been redescribed as oneself that the liberal is able to be "sensitive" to the question of cruelty and humiliation. This act of redescription is still an attempt to appropriate others, only here it is made to sound as if it were a generous act. It is an attempt to make an act of consumption appear to be an act of acknowledgement. (hooks, 1992, p. 13)

According to Scaap, efforts of white people to participate in acts of tolerance and acceptance can be acts of false generosity born of our inability, our lack of understanding, or our guilt. Audre Lorde (1984) echoes this point when she says, "Guilt is only another form of objectification" (p. 132). As white people then, we may care what happens to others, yet be ignorant about what they may need and why they may be angry.

In the case of many of my white students, it is not that there has been no recognition of the pain and anger of the "other"; rather, the pain and anger of the other has been reduced to what they know. Unfortunately, what they know is limited.

Guilt and anxiety may be felt and then projected onto others when it is pointed out to students that some people of color may be angry about their circumstances. Individuals from that group may be seen as the source of discomfort, receiving the projected blame and anger of whites. Nevertheless, Helms (1990) suggests that it is relatively easy for whites to become stuck with their fear and anger, particularly if avoidance of people of color is possible.

■ The Relationship Between Beliefs and Action

The issue of empathy is even further complicated by the fact that beliefs can create a false sense of involvement just as empathy can. According to the social psychology literature, a stronger relationship between attitudes and behavior has been found when the attitude is based on actual experience rather than just imagined situations (Fazio & Zanna, 1981). In addition, norms have a significant influence on the attitude-behavior relationship. For example, the following three norms have been found to influence the relation between our attitudes and behavior:

1. How our immediate community values or rewards certain beliefs
2. Whether we will have anonymity or protection for taking risks in our community
3. Whether our beliefs are personally meaningful to us

For example, although a person may have a strong attitude about a particular subject, he or she may be reluctant to put this attitude into practice due to the community's contrary views or prohibitions (Azjen, 1982; Fazio, 1986; Fazio & Zanna, 1981).

In a racially homogeneous college community, the community norms are such that students question whether they should talk about race at all. Gaertner and Dovidio (1981) have highlighted the tension between caring and action. They claim that whites who believe that they are not prejudiced usually act positively when norms are clear but may not when the environment is more ambiguous. Speaking about or for other racial groups in the presence of an absence may place a student in what they perceive to be a vulnerable position, speaking about something that the community may not value or think is relevant.

Students in one of my classes in teacher education have responded in a poll (written, anonymous) I conducted with 33 students as to why they thought that Martin Luther King's birthday is not considered a legal holiday as yet in New Hampshire. The most given answer (88%) was because there were "no black people" in New Hampshire, and therefore, residents are unsure why they need to recognize a public figure whom they claim is not important "to the majority of the state" (New Hampshire has one of the lowest black populations in the country); three (9%) respondents stated that merchants in the state would not want to lose a day of business; and one person (3%) pronounced that "people in New Hampshire are racists."

During the discussion after the responses were tallied, one student commented that any one of these stances represented a "form of racism," a comment met with much hostility from his classmates. We proceeded to explore his claim by referring back to our definition of racism as a system of advantage based on race, but some students still resisted his accusation, whereas others did not want to get involved. It surprised me that only one student was willing to say it was racist even though many others often wrote privately about their own insights into the workings of racism. This led me to wonder what is at work that prevented other students from seeing and naming racism in a public way.

The fact that normative constraints seem to affect the relationship between attitude and behavior indicates that the relationship between attitude and behavior must be analyzed in context.

In my own work with students on this campus, I have found that if students get to the point of naming the sources of their own racist biographies, they often begin to realize that we learn racism from people we love and respect. Just the naming of this is often felt as a betrayal of one's family. Students who are at this point will privatize their fears of betrayal in journal writings that may or may not be shared with the teacher, or will only discuss their feelings with the teacher in the privacy of the teacher's office, which is a way of showing involvement in the class but is a way that begs off from going public with such admissions. What should be the central texts of the antiracist, critical classroom goes underground and takes the form of furtive confessions (Rosenberg, 1997).

■ Being "Disloyal to Civilization"

One explanation for white students going underground with their insights into their own racism and the racism of others is the tension one experiences in relation to one's own people on a number of levels, not just in relation to one's own immediate family.

James Baldwin (1985) speaks of the paradox of education in his "Talk to Teachers." He points out that "precisely at the point when you begin to develop a conscience, you must find yourself at war with your society" (p. 11). He is referring to his understanding of "identity" in America, which he insists is "a series of myths about one's heroic ancestors." Baldwin raises the question of how we deal with a growing awareness of the many lies on which our country's history is built. According to Beverly Tatum, understanding racism as a system of advantage presents a "serious challenge" to the idea of America as a just society (Tatum, 1992). Understandably, this contradiction often creates discomfort in our students and ourselves.

To address this contradiction and move students beyond empathy toward critique and action around issues of race and racism, I have begun to explore different ways of thinking about how to help students understand the oppression of others without assuming that everyone's experience is the same. Toward this end, I have been working with the following five approaches:

First: Be prepared to own and share with your students your own biography around race and racism. We must all practice being vulnerable in the classroom if we are to do this work. Asking students to share their narratives in general while I, as the teacher, keep silent would be exercising power in a potentially coercive way. And yet, the mere offering up of one's own narrative as a teacher carries with it an unanticipated weight, a gift that places a burden on the receiver. Given the realities of institutional life, mutual self-disclosure in the teacher-student relationship is not truly possible without quite a bit of negotiation (Rosenberg, 1997). It involves entering into a quirky dance with our students, perhaps central to any teacher-student relationship that involves the negotiation of power and authority around classroom rules and the curriculum.

Freezing a pedagogical moment of class time to explain how you may struggle as a teacher is an example of this. You might discuss what went into a decision to use a specific reading, why you may choose to interrupt the class syllabus to discuss something in the news, or why you have responded in a certain way to a student's point. Whenever I freeze the moment, I try to tell the class what I am doing and comment on my own behavior. An example of this is when David (the Asian American student in the classroom scenario given earlier) offered his observation about how the student presenters of *Boyz N' the Hood* did not put the film in a context so that the class would recognize the youths in the film as black and living in a violence-torn community. Without this context, adolescent stress is diffused into a watered-down event. I found it meaningful that the one person who recognized publicly the class's color-blindness is the only student in the class who is not white, and I said so. I shared with them my decision-making process around whether or not to intervene during the student presentation and the messages that may or may not be lost regarding race and teaching if I keep silent.

Marilyn Cochran-Smith (1995) uses the term *uncertain allies* to characterize the uncertainty of preservice teachers and teacher educators who are struggling to understand these issues within themselves and in relation to each other. It is useful to consider her words in light of the issue of teacher vulnerability and what is possible given the realities of institutional life. She suggests that,

> As teachers of and through critical pedagogy, whether our students are children or adults, the best we can do is openly admit our convictions and own our agendas. Then we must acknowledge the fact that if we influence students' views about race and teaching, it is not because we open their eyes to the truth, but to a great extent because we use professional status and personal charisma to persuade them of the perspectives we believe will support their efforts for justice through the orchestration of readings, written assignments, discussion topics, and school experiences. (p. 562)

Second: Invite students to share with each other their confusion, fear, anger, and desire in learning about race and racism. Too often, the experience of becoming a teacher is seen as an individual struggle, not a collective one. Much of the discomfort that white students may experience in the early stages of developing their racial identity is privatized in personal writings to the teacher or hallway or office conferences. These musings and questions should actually be the central texts of the class. Discover ways to include all student concerns and discomforts, even if they are received anonymously at first. I have found that there is a common thread through many of these students' writings about their feelings about race, usually having to do with their families.

I have found that using student narratives from previous terms anonymously works best with helping classes appreciate the commonality of their experiences around race, especially regarding the collective shame of having racist relatives. After getting students' permission from the term(s) before, I distribute anonymous narratives as either a core reading for the class or for individual students to respond to in writing. I have found this to be effective when I teach a large class of 25 to 30 students. Because of the trust factor, it is difficult to have students self-disclosing what they perceive to be unpopular opinions or negative emotions in a large class.

Some key articles on these issues have proven to be important to students in my educational psychology classroom for helping them to begin to develop a language for how to talk about race and racism and their own positionality. Peggy McIntosh's (1989) list of "White Privileges" provides students an opportunity to read together reminders of how much we take for granted as white people. Students may be asked to consider, for example, if they agree with statements such as, "I am never asked to speak for all the people of my racial group" or "I can choose blemish cover or bandages in 'flesh' color and have them more or less match my skin." It is hard for white students not to admit that they have taken some of these privileges for granted, no matter how superficial items on the list may appear on the surface. What is especially useful for students is McIntosh's distinction between prejudice, on the one hand, as "individual acts of kindness or meanness," and racism, on the other, as the invisible "knapsack" of unearned privileges and disadvantages embedded in our entire system. Christine Sleeter (1994) has documented her concern and experience with students regarding white silence on white racism in her piece, *Multicultural Education, Social Positionality, and Whiteness.* Her main argument is that white people generally frame racial issues in ways that are congruent with our own positions, experiences, and vested interests. This paper provides students with a challenge to think about what that means for them and helps them try and understand some of their own anger, frustration, and resistance in learning about race and racism. And Lisa Delpit's (1988) writing about the "culture of power" argues that whether we like it or not, there is a culture of power that operates according to certain codes that children from dominant racial and cultural groups often come to school already knowing better than other children who are not from those groups.

Third: Encourage students not to make themselves ahistorical in the telling of their own biographies around race and racism. For students to become critical thinkers about themselves as preservice teachers, they need to unpack the teacher socialization process they are experiencing as white students in a predominantly white teacher education program. Here I differentiate between what it means to be critical "of," or to stand outside of what one is learning, in contrast to the more ideal stance of what it means to be critical "within," or to stand in relation to one's own knowledge claims, experience, and meaning (Rosenberg, 1989).

By inviting students to write autobiographical narratives about their own experiences with various forms of inequity and access in school, white students are in a much better position to analyze and understand the oppression of others without assuming that everyone's experience is the same if they are required to explore the context for their own experience first as white students. For example, if a student is writing in response to Rist's article about tracking and the self-fulfilling prophecy, I ask them to explore a variety of contexts for that experience (e.g., their age, gender, motivation, school environment, community norms, home environment, historical circumstances, etc.).

This idea of having white students interrogate their own biases and the bias of much of the curriculum in U.S. schools has been suggested by the work of Asante (1991), who explains the notion of "centricity" in education as follows:

> In education centricity refers to a perspective that involves locating students within the context of their own cultural references so that they can relate socially and psychologically to other cultural perspectives. . . . The centrist paradigm is supported by research showing that the most productive method of teaching any student is to place his or her group within the center of the context of knowledge. (p. 171)

A centric view of education would call for white students in this case to come to see other groups as significant in history and influence while recognizing their own perspectives. Because for white students, almost all of their experiences in school sit under a white umbrella, the first step is to have them begin to interrogate their whiteness.

Leslie Roman (1993) insists that "white is a color" when she points out that white culture is the "hidden norm" against which all other racially subordinate groups' so-called "differences" are measured. The very term "white" can imply that whites are "colorless," thereby lacking any "racial subjectivities, interests or privileges" (p. 71). This thinking may result in whites feeling exonerated from any responsibility to challenge racism. This piece is central to students learning how to share critically their educational biographies.

Fourth: Develop opportunities for students to take some form of action based on their developing awareness of race and racism. By this, I do not mean partial interventions or token actions that may only serve to reinforce stereotypes. There is much that could be done within the university community or the local public school system. Nevertheless, valuable learning also happens when students teach each other in their own preservice classrooms within the teacher education program. This happens through group study and presentations and research. Writing for the student newspaper or local newspaper is also a way to take action.

Fifth: Do what you can to achieve a literal presence of the absent group(s) so that students may live and work in relation to others. Crossing geographical borders for preservice teachers to develop exchange opportunities, especially around student teaching, is ideal. It is the only logical solution for how preservice teachers may learn to become successful with culturally diverse students.

■ Conclusion

Adrienne Rich (1978) encourages us to continue to name and dismantle institutions that keep the lie of racism [and sexism] alive, even if it means being "disloyal to civilization." This sounds like a tall order. But we need to help preservice teachers understand that every day in their lives as teachers they may make choices about pedagogy and curriculum that can reinforce or interrupt institutional life that keeps racism and sexism alive. Classroom management, assessment, lesson planning, ordering materials, career advising, the motivation of students are some of the activities that teachers engage in with students that may send strong messages about their worth and possibility.

Kim Chernin (1993) reminds us that we tend to withdraw in the face of enormous social problems, feeling that there is little any of us can do.

Her notion of "the politics of the small" shows the importance of seem-ingly small gestures toward understanding and care and recognizes that people may participate in their own way. She speaks of behavior derived from the politics of the "individual." She describes this behavior as "the personally significant small acts of engagement in which you do what is a natural expression of your own temperament, without having to be-lieve that you are going to change the world" (p. 17). So it is not the size of our contribution to improving our world that is at issue here, but the nature of our contribution. For white preservice teachers to stand in a predominantly white classroom and participate in a conversation with white peers about race and racism and their place in it is an important moment for our students in their teacher socialization process. Never-theless, we must be prepared to acknowledge that opening the unset-tling discourse about race, racism, and teaching in the preservice cur-riculum in the presence of an absence can ultimately only take us so far.

■ Note

1. As of this writing, New Hampshire currently recognizes January 15th (the day of Martin Luther King's birthday) as "Civil Rights Day." Opponents to King's birthday being recognized as a legal holiday in New Hampshire insist that aspects of King's life do not merit holding him as a hero or, moreover, that it is more important to celebrate the idea of civil rights rather than the individ-ual most connected with it. New Hampshire is a fiercely independent state whose resistance to recognizing King's birthday itself as a legal holiday is often seen as an affront to political correctness. Nevertheless, there is growing sup-port for this move. Unfortunately, a proposal this year to turn Civil Rights Day into Martin Luther King Day was acknowledged and supported by the gover-nor but failed to pass legislature by one vote.

■ References

Asante, M. K. (1991). The Afro-centric idea in education. *Journal of Negro Edu-cation, 62,* 170-180.

Azjen, I. (1982). On behaving in accordance with one's attitudes. In M. P. Zanna, E. T. Higgins, & C. P. Herman (Eds.), *Consistency in social behavior: The On-tario symposium, Vol. 2* (pp. 3-15). Hillsdale, NJ: Lawrence Erlbaum.

Baldwin, J. (1985). A talk to teachers. In *The price of the ticket.* New York: St. Martin's.

Boler, M. (1994, March). The risks of empathy: Interrogating multiculturalism's gaze. In *Educational theory*, Paper presented at the Philosophy of Education Society, Charlotte, NC.

Britzman, D. (1991). Decentering discourses in teacher education: Or, the unleashing of unpopular things. *Journal of Education, 173*(3), 60-80.

Chernin, K. (1993). The politics of the small. *Tikkun, 8*(5), 15-18, 91.

Cochran-Smith, M. (1995). Uncertain allies: Understanding the boundaries of race and teaching. *Harvard Educational Review, 65*(4), 541-570.

Delpit, L. (1988). The silenced dialogue: Power and pedagogy in educating other people's children. *Harvard Educational Review, 58*, 280-298.

Fazio, R. H. (1986). How do attitudes guide behavior? In R. M. Sorentino & E. T. Higgins (Eds.), *Handbook of motivation and cognition: Foundations of social behavior* (pp. 204-243). New York: Guilford.

Fazio, R. H., & Zanna, M. P. (1981). Direct experience and attitude-behavior consistency. In L. Berkowitz (Ed.), *Advances in experimental social psychology* (Vol. 14, pp. 161-202). New York: Academic Press.

Fine, M. (1985). Dropping out of high school: An inside look. *Social Policy, 16*, 43-50.

Gaertner, S. L., & Dovidio, J. F. (1981). Racism among the well-intentioned. In E. G. Clausen & B. J. Bermingham (Eds.), *Pluralism, racism, and public policy: The search for equality*. Boston: G. K. Hall.

Gilmore, P. (1985). 'Gimme room': School resistance, attitude, and access to literacy. *Journal of Education, 167*(1), 111-128.

Hall, S. (1992). The question of cultural identity. In S. Hall, D. Held, & T. McGrew (Eds.), *Modernity & its futures* (pp. 273-316). Cambridge, UK: Polity.

Helms, J. E. (Ed.). (1990). *Black and white racial identity: Theory, research, and practice*. Westport, CT: Greenwood.

hooks, b. (1992). *Black looks/Race and representation*. Boston: South End Press.

Lorde, A. (1984). *Sister outsider*. New York: Crossing.

McIntosh, P. (1989). White privilege: Unpacking the invisible knapsack. *Peace & Freedom, 49*(4), 10-12.

Noddings, N. (1984). *Caring*. Berkeley: University of California Press.

Rich, A. (1978). Disloyal to civilization: Feminism, racism, gynephobia. In *On lies, secrets, and silence*. New York: Norton.

Rist, R. C. (1970). Student social class and teacher expectations: The self-fulfilling prophecy in ghetto education. *Harvard Educational Review, 40*(3), 411-450.

Roman, L. G. (1993). White is a color! White defensiveness, postmodernism, and anti-racist pedagogy. In C. McCarthy & W. Crichlow (Eds.), *Race, identity, and representation in education*. New York: Routledge.

Rosenberg, P. M. (1989). *The empowerment educator as disguised ruler: The paradox of negotiating power and status in a college classroom*. Unpublished doctoral dissertation, University of Pennsylvania, Philadelphia.

Rosenberg, P. M. (1997). Underground discourses: Exploring whiteness in teacher education. In M. Fine, L. Weis, L. Powell, & M. Wong (Eds.), *Off white: Readings on race, power and society.* New York: Routledge.

Sleeter, C. E. (1994, April). *Multicultural education, social positionality, and whiteness.* Paper presented at the American Educational Research Association, New Orleans, LA.

Tatum, B. D. (1992). Talking about race, learning about racism: An application of racial identity development theory in the classroom. *Harvard Educational Review, 62*(1), 1-24.

Tatum, B. D. (1994). Teaching White students about racism: The search for White allies and the restoration of hope. *Teachers College Record, 95,* 462-476.

Confronting Issues of Race and Power in the Culture of Schools

A Case Study of a Preservice Teacher

■ *Jane Agee*

The preservice teaching experience is a crucial time in the rite of passage into the profession of teaching. This ritual of initiation, frequently depicted as a gauntlet by university teachers and by preservice students themselves, inspires many fears and concerns. For LaTasha Wages, an African American preservice student, this rite of passage held even greater challenges than for the majority of her white, middle-class peers.

This chapter, part of a larger case study (Agee, 1994), addresses LaTasha's concerns and expectations about her preservice teaching, her relationship with her cooperating teachers, her experiences with the culture of the school during her preservice teaching, and her reflections in June 1993, after her preservice teaching experience.

Although very little published research has appeared in mainstream journals on African American preservice teachers and their socialization into the profession of teaching, King (1991, 1993) and others (Franklin, 1987; Graham, 1987; Irvine, 1988) have called for more attention to the

AUTHOR'S NOTE: All names of people in this case study are pseudonyms.

problems of recruitment and retention of teachers of African American heritage. King's (1993) review of research on the declining numbers of minority teachers reveals many potential obstacles, from limited financial aid and traditionally low pay scales for teachers to issues such as teacher competency tests and licensing procedures. However, the present study reveals other less obvious obstacles for a preservice teacher of color.

Britzman (1986) observed that preservice teachers often encounter student teaching practices that represent an unexamined "ideological education" and that promote "particular images of power, knowledge, and values by rewarding particular forms of individual and institutional behavior" (p. 443). Conversely, those practices can be punitive toward those whose race, ethnicity, or values do not cohere with the institutional ideology or the culture of the school. Graham (1993) found that issues of power in the preservice experience, especially the gender issues that emerged from a relationship (in this case, between a female student teacher who questioned the assumptions of her male cooperating teacher), created a source of dissonance that nearly destroyed any possibility of dialogue and collegiality.

When a preservice teacher enters a school to begin student teaching, he or she steps into a complex culture driven by politics of power and ideology. The stance of a student teacher, as an outsider, is precarious from the beginning. It is not surprising that Sperling (1994) found the narratives of student teachers were filled with metaphors for battle: "Battles, contests, are central, and they are of wills, ideas, behaviors, as teachers and students engage in such ways that only one comes out the winner" (p. 151). As the story of LaTasha makes clear, this ideological battlefield with its hierarchy of power can become particularly threatening and debilitating for a preservice teacher of color.

■ Data Sources

Data included eight audiotaped interviews with LaTasha and one with each of her cooperating teachers, videotapes of LaTasha teaching on two consecutive days in a class of ninth graders, field notes made during observations of her teaching in other classes, field notes on weekly field-center seminars, and documents such as lesson plans and copies of the planning log that she kept during her preservice teaching.

■ LaTasha Wages

LaTasha was a 21-year-old undergraduate in English education at the time of this study. She was proud of her African American heritage and her family and described what she wanted in her own future in terms of her parents' achievements:

> They worked hard for what they have, and they both are successes in their lives, and they have a lot of material things. They are very blessed with that. I also want that for my family. . . . So I am ambitious, and I do want the kind of lifestyle that I have been accustomed to all throughout my life, even as a child. I want my kids not to have to want for anything, and I'm not saying they'll get everything they want, but they'll never go hungry. I've never known what it was like to have my lights turned off or my phone turned off. (01/22/93)

LaTasha's parents were important in shaping her self-perception and self-esteem. In our January interview, she said, "My parents always taught me to be proud of myself. They always taught me to never let people run over me, and so that's why I think a lot of times, I'm very outspoken." Her confidence about who she was, she said, helped her to maintain her identity:

> Some people tend to lose their identity if they're in the minority in a group and especially if they're attending a university or a college that way. Still, I attend school with those of European descent, and I don't have problems with it, but I still maintain my sense of identity. (01/22/93)

Her family and religious values were a continuing source of strength and informed her strong sense of commitment to becoming a teacher throughout her preservice experience. She also had an amazing reservoir of courage and determination that helped her overcome obstacles that might have defeated the ordinary person. It was not surprising that she identified with the character Mama, "a woman who dares to hold steadfast to her dreams," in the play *A Raisin in the Sun* (Hansberry, 1959).

■ Early Expectations and Concerns

One of LaTasha's early concerns about her preservice teaching centered on the racial makeup of Sanders County schools and her role within a largely white school system. LaTasha saw her role as a teacher in moral terms. As Lyons (1990) pointed out, "the new rhetoric of teacher voice argues that it is above all characterized not only by knowledge but also by a tacit sense of mission, one that creates conflict for teachers" (p. 161). The conflict for LaTasha was complex. She had a deep desire to help African American students: "I would prefer teaching African American students because I see that there is a need there." Yet she worried that "people will think that if I'm thrown in a room, or I'm teaching in a county that is a majority white, . . . that I really won't care because that's not where my heart is." She countered this imaginary scenario quietly and firmly, "That's not the type of person I am."

Fordham (1993), an African American English teacher, addressed this same issue. Like LaTasha, she affirmed her own identity while making clear her stance on teaching: "As a teacher, my dedication to teach all students as they are is essential to my instructional practices" (p. 87). Fordham, again like LaTasha, saw her "strong sense of self" and "cultural history" as assets: "By acknowledging and accepting my own identity, I am able to accept others and assist my students, whoever they are, in building their own identities as readers, writers, and human beings" (p. 87).

LaTasha addressed these issues in her letter to a yet-unknown cooperating teacher. In early January, LaTasha's university supervisor asked the preservice students in the methods and curriculum classes to each assemble a portfolio to present to their cooperating teachers and to write a letter describing themselves and their goals for teaching. In an excerpt from her letter, LaTasha describes both her experiences as an African American and her moral stance on teaching all students:

> It has been my unfortunate experience as a student and in the work-force to have some teachers and people try and make me feel inadequate or inferior for no apparent reason other than that particular person's ignorance. I know that this has been the experience of many students in the educational system as well. I want to give all of my students a sense of pride and self-worth. I want them to recognize that they do not have to remain stagnant in their lives, for they are all capable of achieving. Knowledge is theirs to claim, and I simply

want to help them define what they want out of life and perhaps motivate others who do not believe that they are capable of achieving personal success. (Letter to cooperating teachers, 01/15/93)

In her letter, she was both reflective and pragmatic: "I recognize that I cannot save the world, and I am interested in seeing how my views change as time progresses. However, as a future teacher, I have to love what I am doing."

Early Expectations of Cooperating Teachers

Before LaTasha ever met her cooperating teachers, she had several specific expectations about the kind of relationship she wanted with them. When I interviewed her in early February, just after she had found out who her cooperating teachers would be, she said she wanted "a happy medium" in her relationships with them:

> This is something very new for me, so I think it would be foolish if I try to say that I want total autonomy and I do whatever I want. I think that I want someone who is willing to let me kind of like set the pace, and they can help me in the beginning and start letting me kind of go out on my own. (02/09/93)

Her desire for some initial guidance was tempered by her desire to be independent. She felt having the cooperating teacher in the classroom with her could be helpful "the first or second time I do an exercise," but she realized how such an arrangement could undermine her role:

> I don't want their presence in there all the time because then it's really like I'm just sort of like a substitute teacher, and I'm performing for that teacher that is sitting in the back of the class as opposed to me actually trying to learn about the students and interact.

LaTasha also wanted her cooperating teachers to help her with planning, teaching strategies, and resources. In her initial letter in January to her cooperating teachers, she said, "I hope that you will allow me [to] 'pillage, rob, and steal' your ideas, because I am a novice, and I do need guidance." She was particularly interested in getting some guidance from her cooperating teachers on bringing multicultural literature into the classes. She said if a piece of literature were not in the course curriculum, "I would ask my cooperating teacher or head of the department, 'Do you think this is okay if I use this particular short story? Is it appropriate for ninth or tenth grade . . . ?' " Although her expectations were modest and very typical of those of other preservice students, they became part of a covert conflict with one of her cooperating teachers.

■ The Context of the School

After visiting Armstrong High School one day a week during the month of February, LaTasha actually began her preservice teaching there in March 1993. Her university supervisor, aware of LaTasha's concern about being placed in a predominately white school, placed her at Armstrong High School because, unlike many of the Sanders County schools, this high school had a racially diverse population. Armstrong, located in a large metropolitan area, drew students from middle-class and lower-middle-class neighborhoods. The older one-story brick school, which had far outgrown its original building, was composed of a maze of breezeways connecting wing after wing of added classrooms. In contrast to many of the newer schools in the county with the latest architectural amenities, Armstrong seemed worn and cramped. However, LaTasha was pleased with her assignment. Her fears about teaching in a Sanders County school seemed to subside once she visited her cooperating teachers and her future students. Perhaps because her cooperating teachers were white, as were most of the teachers in the school, she was particularly pleased that her university supervisor had asked a young African American teacher at Armstrong to be her mentor. Her relationship with her mentor helped her to survive the difficulties she encountered during her student teaching, both with her cooperating teachers and with the faculty.

■ The Cooperating Teacher–Preservice Teacher Relationship

As Britzman (1991) noted, "individual notions of power privatize contradictions and thereby thwart those learning to teach from theorizing about and effectively intervening in such contradictory realities" (p. 60). For LaTasha, those "notions of power" threatened her conceptions of teaching and her efforts to assume the status of teacher. As a result, her preservice teaching experience gradually became a battle for survival. The battle lines were drawn not by her students but by her powerful cooperating teachers, one of whom tried to sabotage LaTasha's role as a teacher and by other faculty members who marginalized LaTasha rather than offering her collegiality and mentoring.

Frieda Manning

Frieda Manning, a veteran teacher, was head of the English Department at Armstrong High School at the time of this study. LaTasha worked with two of Frieda Manning's 10th-grade academic (average) level classes. Frieda had a long-standing reputation for excellence in her own teaching and in her departmental leadership; however, she suffered from a severe, undiagnosed health problem during the Spring of 1993 that affected her behavior in general in late Spring. I interviewed Frieda on May 18, 1993, just prior to a diagnosis and subsequent surgery. Our interview was brief and tense as she had forgotten that I was coming and quite naturally had more important things with which to contend. However, the data from this interview are helpful in describing her perceptions of LaTasha.

LaTasha had described Frieda Manning as "a very strict person" with "rules" and "procedures" in an interview in late March, and Frieda confirmed LaTasha's observations. She described herself as "very structured" and said that she was impressed with LaTasha because she, too, was "very organized, very structured." Frieda admired LaTasha's ability to handle potential discipline problems effectively:

> I think, as with all teacher candidates, they [the students] thought that might mean a holiday vacation, and she let them know very quickly—which I told her was one of the smartest things she'd ever do, she established herself, established her rules, didn't take any foolishness, started off day one.

She said the students respected LaTasha "as the teacher," something she found lacking in previous preservice teachers: "Many times, that is the hardest thing to convince a teacher candidate of, that you've got to be tough . . . you've got to put on a facade."

Frieda also praised LaTasha for her ability to work well with teenagers. She felt she was a "very, very good teacher" and pointed to her strengths in closing:

She is very prepared. She desires to share her knowledge with the students. She requires that they respond to her in a positive, courteous manner, and she requires them to treat each other that way. . . . I see many, many good things. Her level of maturity amazes me. She's definitely not the typical college senior getting out.

When I interviewed LaTasha on March 3, 1993, she had just taken over full teaching responsibilities for Frieda Manning's classes. She explained that she had not had any real problems with discipline in Frieda's two classes: "I just eased on in and just kept her rules, so it's very easy, and they know what to expect already." At this point in her relationship with Frieda Manning, LaTasha seemed comfortable with her own role, but she still called Frieda "Mrs. Manning" and continued to do so thereafter.

Frieda Manning's illness later caused her to have severe problems, such as headaches and what LaTasha described as "mood swings," which affected her relationship with LaTasha and with other colleagues. However, LaTasha liked Frieda Manning and in June was able to put the tense moments into perspective:

I just basically let it all that roll off my back because of that [her illness]. Other people could tell her mood swings, and I wasn't the only one who got it from Mrs. Manning. Teachers, she and teachers had it out.

In spite of the problems caused by Frieda Manning's illness, LaTasha liked her approach:

With Mrs. Manning's class, I knew what she wanted me to teach—poetry, short story, and novel. That's what she told me. That was my guideline, and I did it, and I felt I had more ownership in that class.

She also valued her honest approach to their relationship: "I liked Mrs. Manning because Mrs. Manning was straightforward." She said, "Whenever we had a problem, we talked about it." However, LaTasha never enjoyed a collegial relationship with Frieda Manning. LaTasha's status remained that of a visiting college student, a status confirmed by an incident (described later in this chapter) in late May after LaTasha had signed a contract with another school system.

Elaine Newton

In addition to her assignment with Frieda Manning, LaTasha was assigned to Elaine Newton, who had two ninth-grade vocational educa-tion classes, because LaTasha had specifically requested an opportunity to work with remedial students. Elaine had been teaching for 23 years, both in rural schools and in the metropolitan area where she now lived and taught. More than half the students were African American and had a history of severe difficulties with academic work. The two classes were small, with about 10 students in each class, about half the number of those who had started the year.

From the beginning, LaTasha had some reservations about Elaine and the vocational classes. In our interview in late February, after she had made some initial visits to Armstrong, LaTasha voiced some con-cerns about Elaine and her attitude toward the ninth-grade vocational students: "I was a little resistant to her just because I thought that they were limiting, um, the kids' abilities, because most of the kids in those classes are minority students." LaTasha blamed society and the institu-tion of school for the kind of tracking that she saw in the vocational classes:

> I hate the word minority, but most of the kids are not of European descent, or not white students, and um, some of the things that they suggested, I didn't like. Like, um, limiting the kids to vocation. I re-alize that everybody won't go to college, but then to say that "All you will ever do is clean up at a hotel . . . " I have problems with that.

However, LaTasha was willing to give Elaine the benefit of the doubt at this early point in their relationship:

> But now I've seen the kids more, and I think she really cares about the kids, and perhaps I misunderstood her. . . . I don't think she wants to limit the students. . . . I think she tries to be more realistic in knowing the kids are probably not going to go to college—which is true. They probably won't.

When I interviewed LaTasha at the end of March, Elaine Newton sat in the room. When I suggested that we go elsewhere to avoid disturbing Elaine, Elaine said we were not bothering her, and LaTasha laughed and said her presence was not a problem. At this time (about four weeks into her preservice teaching), LaTasha felt very positive about her relationships with Frieda Manning and Elaine Newton: "I have two wonderful master teachers who definitely have control of their classes and know what they are doing." Unfortunately, LaTasha's euphoria was short-lived. During the subsequent weeks at Armstrong, the relationship between LaTasha and Elaine slowly began to unravel. At the heart of their dissonance were issues of race and power.

In May, when I interviewed Elaine, what emerged was a covert struggle on her part to protect and maintain her own relationship with the two classes of vocational ninth graders (nearly all African American) assigned to LaTasha. In response to my question about LaTasha's potential as a teacher, Elaine immediately focused on her own expectations that LaTasha would be "popular" and LaTasha's problems:

> I expected LaTasha to be very popular with my remedial students, and she has not been. She has had a terrible struggle. She's had to give many, many detentions, and students who were no problem for me end up being problems for her. And we are trying to deal with that, and part of that, of course, is her age.

Elaine had set up a covert competition with LaTasha, and the messages in this interview suggested there was no way LaTasha could win. Ironically, Elaine complimented LaTasha for her ability to go about her teaching in spite of what she believed the students' attitude toward her to be: "It doesn't concern me that they don't like her; um, I think that is admirable that this is not a concern of hers, to be their friend because particularly with remedial ninth grade, you don't cross that one [laughs]." She came back to the issue of popularity when she situated LaTasha in relation to herself and Frieda Manning:

> And it is also difficult. She took over two classes from old pros with their students. Now, if my students hated me and she came in, she might be more popular. Also I have had my students all year, which is unusual.

Elaine consistently described her relationship with these students as positive and LaTasha's relationship with them as negative. When she posited the reasons for the students' behavior, she situated herself in an unassailable position of power:

They are very comfortable with me . . . and I'm more of a mother figure to them than LaTasha is. And, um, somehow they have perceived in her a threat . . . or they have been rude to her. Outright rude. And, um, I have not felt that, and I think it's my age. I'm old enough to be their mother or their grandmother [laughs] in some cases, and her youth is something that seems to frighten them. With remedial kids, they are always, "Is she going to embarrass me? Is she going to call on me to read and make fun of my efforts?"—that kind of thing [she seems to catch herself here] and LaTasha has not done that. (05/18/93)

Although Elaine believed LaTasha represented some sort of threat to the students, she never identified that threat, except to suggest that it might have been her age. Elaine's strong conception of herself as a mother figure to the students left no room for LaTasha to develop a relationship with these students and to establish herself as their teacher. Her tenacity in protecting this relationship became clear when she talked about her agreeing to allow LaTasha to work with these two classes: "She [LaTasha] requested a remedial program. I *never* give up my remedial kids unless someone really wants them because it's not fair to either one."

Elaine also criticized LaTasha for her lack of enthusiasm in her delivery. She said, "She expresses more enthusiasm for a unit when she is planning it and when she is telling me about it than she gets across to the class." She first attributed this anomaly to fear:

It's fear and all new, but, um, when I had to take over for her with my ninth grade remedial, um, they seemed to feel . . . They said to me, "You like the book better than she does." Well, that's not true at all. It's just that I know that if I'm excited about it, they'll be excited about it. (05/18/93)

Elaine then attributed LaTasha's lack of enthusiasm to her personality, a less remediable factor:

LaTasha has a very laid-back personality, and as a result, the lessons tend to lack enthusiasm and spunk. They are ho-hum, humdrum, particularly with remedial students. You have to build a fire under them, send off rockets, do double back flips, particularly at the end of the year. (05/18/93)

When I asked her if she had talked with LaTasha about this problem, she returned to the issue of personality in such a way that implied there was nothing else to say: "Now, it is very difficult to manufacture that [enthusiasm] if that is not part of your personality." Again, Elaine framed herself as expert and successful and LaTasha as both inexperienced and deficient.

Not only did Elaine set herself up as an expert knower and "old pro," but she also made clear her desire to protect her status and power. She never talked about specific ways she might share that expertise and power. In fact, she seemed to resent LaTasha's efforts to solicit her help. Elaine complained, "One of her weaknesses is . . . that she wants me to tell her the units that I have done." She reasoned that LaTasha should be more independent:

> And I understand that with a student teacher—I don't expect them to reinvent the wheel. That's ridiculous, but some of it needs to be their ideas. Um, she's a little timid to come up with, or she lacks the imagination to come up with . . . I insisted that the last unit be hers. Well, she called other teachers to get it! [laughs] (05/18/93)

Even when Elaine praised LaTasha, she tempered her praise with criticism or offered contradictory assessments of LaTasha's strategies. For example, she praised LaTasha for her "flexibility"—"She sees a sinking ship, and she does something about it."—but the implication was that LaTasha frequently had to deal with a "sinking ship" scenario. The following excerpt from our interview illustrates the contradictory nature of Elaine's remarks particularly well:

> Her overall goals are wonderful on paper. I don't know how well she communicates them to the kids. I think she was very fond of *Roll of Thunder, Hear My Cry*, but I don't know if it came across to the kids that way, um, that she was excited about this. And when you do have trouble with discipline and respect, it is difficult to be enthusiastic. Um, so I think she will make a fine teacher once she has some experience, um, so I have no reservations in recommending her. I think she's been admirably prepared and I have never asked her to do something that she did not do, so, um, I think she is going to make a good teacher. (05/18/93)

It was not surprising that LaTasha commented on Elaine's "mixed messages" in June.

Lyons (1990) found that

> the teacher's assessment of how to present subject matter is mediated by his or her understanding of students as knowers and is informed by his or her own stance towards a discipline and knowledge as well as consideration of the self as knower. (p. 175)

LaTasha believed that through prayer, family support, and perseverance, she could overcome almost any obstacle or adversity. She also believed literature, especially multicultural literature, offered an antidote to bias and oppression. She wanted to use literature to show students, especially remedial students, that they, too, could both see beyond and overcome their circumstances. However, as she worked with the remedial students, she found unanticipated obstacles to her goals and little support from Elaine.

LaTasha's desire to help and nurture her remedial students created an ethical dilemma for her. With her sixth-period class in particular, LaTasha experienced great frustration. The class, which she described as "predominantly boys," was unresponsive to her efforts to engage them in literature; their peer culture ruled out responding to a teacher: "For me, they're more so in the role of, we have to look cool in front of our friends." Their disrespect for her as their teacher had a profound effect on her stance:

> There are a lot more students in there that challenge me, and you can't . . . I'm learning you can't save everyone, and I think sometimes I leave here frustrated after sixth period because I want to [save them], but I also have to be grounded and realistic, so what I do is, I just say a little prayer in my car on my way home. (03/29/93)

Being "realistic" also involved giving detention to obstreperous students, something LaTasha found especially disturbing. Such punitive actions as giving detentions conflicted with her goals for teaching, yet she understood her culturally defined responsibilities as a teacher:

> I follow the rules, and they have to get detention, but, um, it's because I want everything to be perfect, and I want everybody to learn from me, and I was just like really upset about it, and I could tell, and so I just said a little prayer and said, "Wait a minute, stop, you can't take it home with you all the time. You can't let it be your all and all." (03/29/93)

LaTasha's problems with Elaine and the ninth-grade vocational students intensified during April and May. Although the university supervisor and her graduate assistant were observing LaTasha teach (approximately once every 2 weeks) and being very supportive of her *teaching* strategies, they were unaware of the conflict between Elaine and LaTasha until the end of May. During this time, LaTasha became aware that Elaine was actually trying to subvert her status as teacher and her relationship with the students but was uncertain about why or what to do about it:

> I felt like I was being sabotaged because she would tell me little things that they [the students] would say about me that were kind of like . . . negative, and I'd feel bad, but then they would come in sixth period and say, "Well, hey, what's up Miss Wages. How ya doing?" (06/11/93)

LaTasha also overheard Elaine telling a student, "This is just a student teacher. I'll be in here watching her today." Such comments, LaTasha said, "really angered" her. They were part of an ongoing conflict that LaTasha did not fully understand even after she left Armstrong in June.

■ Tensions Between LaTasha and the Culture of School

This tension between what LaTasha had envisioned for herself as a teacher and the cultural constraints of school became even greater after she began to interact with the faculty at Armstrong High School. The culture of the school, with its nearly all-white faculty, forced LaTasha into the role of outsider. Just as LaTasha's relationships with her cooperating teachers became problematic, her negotiation of the culture of the school also became more difficult.

In our final interview in June, she said she wished Armstrong's faculty "was more diverse" and talked about some of the situations she encountered in the teachers' lounge:

> When you would walk in on conversations that they had on particular students—and I guess I am overly sensitive to anything I think may be racial—and, um, I pick up on certain things that people say, and a lot of times people would sit, and they wouldn't see me come in and their backs would be to me, and one would say, "Shh, shh,

shh!" and they would point at me. I mean how *else* am I supposed to feel when people do things like that? (06/11/93)

When LaTasha was sharing her experiences with a small group of preservice teachers back on campus in June, she said she felt a faculty should be "more cohesive" and should "work together as a unit instead of stabbing each other in the back all the time as soon as you walk out of the lounge." She said she heard "childish things" such as, "Look at what she had on!" after a teacher left the lounge.

LaTasha also shared with her group on campus some of her experiences as an African American preservice teacher working with a predominantly white faculty. Two of those experiences, in particular, angered her. Both occurred in the faculty lounge. The first had to do with the other teachers' perceptions of her as a spokesperson for all African Americans:

> It is like I was the spokesperson because I am black, and it used to irk me. We'd be in the lounge, and then they would start a conversation, and then they would turn to me. There was one lady that made me so angry. . . . She asked me, "How in the world could anyone compare the Jewish Holocaust to slavery?" And she said, "I'm so sick of this. . . . LaTasha! I want to ask you, what do you think?" (06/11/93)

LaTasha's reaction was swift: "I said, 'How dare you put me on the spot like this and ask me to be a spokesman for my race.' " She said she pointed out to this teacher that "it doesn't matter who suffered or who suffered more" and that it was not her place to make such judgments: "It's just that a wrong was committed on both groups of people."

The other experience that LaTasha found reprehensible centered on the teachers' conversations about African American students: "It really angered me to hear them make jokes about kids bringing guns to school and say, 'Well, maybe they'll shoot each other and get them out of my class.' " LaTasha felt that "kids learn by example" and that as teachers, the faculty should "try to do some things to bring them [students of different races] together." LaTasha believed that remaining quiet about such conversations was tantamount to tacit approval or acceptance: "Sometimes, being quiet says that you are agreeing with what is being said." She decided to take "a stand" against such faculty lounge talk: "When a certain group would walk in there, I'd leave, and they knew why I was leaving."

As a novice teacher with goals that centered on nurturing and en-couraging students, LaTasha found such discourse to be at odds with her conception of teaching. She felt faculty who said such things as, "I'm going to get him," about a particular student "didn't care." She found it difficult to believe these teachers were in the profession: "I didn't under-stand why they were even in education." Although she identified one group of teachers who engaged in such negative discourse, she felt the entire faculty lacked the ability to work together in a supportive, col-laborative way.

The crisis point for LaTasha and her two cooperating teachers came in May after she had been hired by North Pines, a large high school in a city about 50 miles away from Sanders County. She was invited by the department head of the English department of North Pines to attend an afternoon meeting where courses for the following year were to be ne-gotiated within the department. Although LaTasha had only missed 2 days because of illness (the preservice teachers were allowed 3 sick days) and had not taken her 2 personal leave days, Elaine and Frieda told her she could not leave Armstrong the last period of the day to go to the meeting at North Pines. LaTasha called on her university super-visor to help her negotiate her one-period leave, but the negotiation was unsuccessful. In the end, LaTasha stood up for herself, told her cooper-ating teachers she had a right to go, and went to the meeting.

During our interview in June, LaTasha tried to sort out her feelings about her cooperating teachers, especially focusing on what had hap-pened with Elaine. LaTasha did not understand why Elaine had treated her the way she had and had not been open with her: "I don't know why she would never tell me except maybe it was a personal vendetta where she really wanted to hurt me." In retrospect, LaTasha said her experience with Elaine was "a dose of reality." On both counts, LaTasha was right. Although LaTasha did not understand the threat she represented to Elaine Newton, she certainly sensed the competitive and vindictive tone of Elaine's behavior. Moreover, what happened with LaTasha and Elaine is unfortunately not unique. Graham (1993) found that power issues were central to all of the cooperating teacher-preservice teacher pairs in her study: "In all of these cases, the student teaching experience was characterized by tensions and dissonances that were difficult for the stu-dent teacher to address directly and often difficult for the cooperating teacher to broach as well" (p. 184).

Although LaTasha did not feel Elaine's behavior was racially moti-vated, it certainly complicated the relationship. Elaine's specific refer-ence to LaTasha's race as being a factor in how "popular" she expected her to be with the vocational students seems to point to an initial fear of having someone else in the classroom that the students might like better. Race also became an issue in terms of their very different perceptions of the vocational students. LaTasha recalled that Elaine "would use words like 'stupid' " to describe her vocational students. LaTasha said Elaine "really feels . . . she is doing the kids a service" but "underestimated their ability." LaTasha was especially disturbed when the students said, "Well, don't you know this is a dumb class and we're not supposed to do things like that?" Thus, race and very different perspectives on the vocational students intensified the usual dissonance that occurs in the complex relationship a preservice teacher must negotiate with a cooperating teacher.

■ Conclusions

Britzman (1986) observed that "the stories of student teachers are charged by their marginality and otherness, and by their individual capacity to empathize with the classroom students' perspectives that continue to be housed in their own subjectivities" (p. 59). What happened with LaTasha and Elaine is unfortunately not unique. Graham (1993) found that power issues were central to all of the cooperating teacher-preservice teacher pairs in her study: "In all of these cases, the student teaching experience was characterized by tensions and dissonances that were difficult for the student teacher to address directly and often difficult for the cooperating teacher to broach as well" (p. 184). The research of King (1991), Fox (1991), Graham (1993), and Agee (1994) confirm Britzman's assessment about preservice teachers' marginality within the culture of school. In each of these case studies, the power wielded by the cooperating teacher and conflicting conceptions of teaching threatened, and often undermined, the purported goal of student teaching: to offer a professionally supported mentorship. For a preservice teacher of color, such power struggles, couched within a culture of school that marginalizes members of minority groups, can be overwhelming. If LaTasha had not had an African American mentor, a supportive family, a caring university supervisor, and a strong desire to overcome obstacles to her professional goals, she might very well have left the profession of teaching.

King (1993) believes that "discussions about diversity in school districts and institutions of higher learning must continue—including the causes, considerations, and consequences of the limited presence of African American teachers" (p. 142). Although it is not possible to generalize from a single case study, the data on LaTasha's experience add urgency not only to the call for continued discussions but also to the need for further case-study research on the experiences of preservice teachers of color.

■ References

Agee, J. (1994). *Readers becoming teachers of literature: A meta-case study of the pre-service experience in a secondary English education program.* Unpublished doctoral dissertation, The University of Georgia, Athens.

Britzman, D. P. (1986). Cultural myths in the making of a teacher: Biography and social structure in teacher education. *Harvard Educational Review, 56,* 442-456.

Britzman, D. P. (1991). *Practice makes practice: A critical study of learning to teach.* Albany: State University of New York Press.

Fordham, S. (1993). "Those loud black girls": (Black) women, silence, and gender "passing" in the academy. *Anthropology and Education Quarterly, 24*(1), 3-32.

Fox, D. L. (1991). *From English major to English teacher: Case studies of student teachers and their first year of teaching English.* Unpublished doctoral dissertation, University of Missouri-Columbia.

Franklin, J. H. (1987). The desperate need for Black teachers. *Change, 19*(3), 44-45.

Graham, P. (1993). Curious positions: Reciprocity and tensions in the student teacher/cooperating teacher relationship. *English Education, 25*(4), 213-230.

Graham, P. A. (1987). Black teachers: A drastically scarce resource. *Phi Delta Kappan, 68*(8), 598-605.

Hansberry, L. (1959). *A raisin in the sun.* New York: Random House.

Irvine, J. J. (1988). An analysis of the problem of the disappearing Black educators. *Elementary School Journal, 88*(5), 503-514.

King, S. H. (1991). *Experiencing the early career experiences of the African-American teaching pool.* Unpublished doctoral dissertation, Columbia University, Teachers College, New York.

King, S. H. (1993). The limited presence of African-American teachers. *Review of Educational Research, 63*(2), 115-149.

Lyons, N. (1990). Dilemmas of knowing: Ethical and epistemological dimensions of teachers' work and development. *Harvard Educational Review, 60*(2), 159-180.

Sperling, M. (1994). Moments remembered, moments displayed: Narratization, metaphor, and the experience of teaching. *English Journal, 26*(3), 142-156.

Teacher Efficacy

How Do Teachers Feel About Their Abilities to Teach African American Students?

- *Valerie Ooka Pang*
- *Velma A. Sablan*

The failure of public education to improve the quality of life for African Americans has been persistent and pervasive. African American children continually trail their European American peers in school achievement. By sixth grade, African American students are generally 2 years behind in reading, math, and in writing skills (Lomotey, 1990). The long-range outcomes of persistent failure have been reflected in the high rates of high school dropouts, teen pregnancy, juvenile delinquency, social welfare, prison incarcerations, AIDS, drug addiction, and unemployment, to name a few. If education is the key to solving critical social problems in the United States, then education has failed African American students.

Educators are quick to point out that there are African Americans who have done well in school and have achieved academic and social success (Ford, 1992; Foster, 1994). Recent studies have described competent African American teachers who have been highly successful with

African American students (Foster, 1994; Irvine, 1990). These studies find the teacher to be a key element in the classroom because teachers can be supportive or unfriendly in their relationships with students. Successful teachers are frequently described as supportive mentors who believe in their students despite predisposing factors, such as poverty (Poplin, 1992). These teachers believe they can reach their students and teach them; they have high levels of efficacy in their abilities as teachers.

This study is important for two reasons. First, though teacher efficacy has been investigated from a general perspective, no study could be located focusing on teacher efficacy as it relates to an underrepresented group. What teachers believe about their abilities to teach children of color may be a critical aspect of teacher training. Stereotypical notions about specific ethnic groups exist in the minds of many teachers (Pang, 1988; Tran, Young, & DiLella, 1994). Teacher training institutions must assist teachers to better understand how their belief systems influence what they do and how they teach children from various nonmainstream ethnic groups (Banks & Banks, 1995; Grant, 1995; Pang, 1994; Sleeter & Grant, 1994; Zeichner, 1993). Second, studies that have explored the continual underachievement of African American students have not focused attention on issues of teacher-student relationships. When the majority of the teaching force in this country is European American and female, the need to look at relationships is obvious. Cultural conflicts may arise when teachers lack knowledge of or hold misconceptions about the African Americans' culture, customs, and values.

The purpose of this study was to investigate how confident pre- service and inservice teachers feel about their skills to teach African American students. Few studies could be located that have investigated teacher efficacy as it relates to students from underrepresented groups. This study examines the theoretical construct of teacher efficacy as it relates to African American students.

■ Teacher Efficacy and African American Students

Teacher efficacy has been found to be a multidimensional construct that includes how confident teachers view their personal abilities to be effective teachers and their expectations about the influence of teaching on student learning. We believe a critical dimension of teacher efficacy, which has not been investigated, is the impact of teacher beliefs about race.

Race is a powerful element in schooling as seen by prevailing attitudes about African Americans. For example, Bowie and Bond (1994) found preservice teachers to exhibit negative attitudes toward Black English. Teachers surveyed believed Black English had a faulty grammar system and felt children who spoke Black English to be less capable than children who spoke standard English. Rubovitz and Maehr (1973) found teachers to have lower expectations and to give less attention to African American students in comparison to European American children. Researchers have also discussed African American families, using a deficit-deficiency paradigm that has assisted in perpetuating negative perceptions of African Americans (Jenkins, 1989).

There are three theoretical models that are used to explain the underachievement of African Americans. The following theories explain the achievement gap from various viewpoints:

The Deficit Theory

Teachers who believe in the deficit model assume African American students lack ability or have had inadequate parenting or both. There is something wrong with the student and his or her home experiences that schools have little control over (Villegas, 1991). Teachers believe African American students have little potential and expect less performance from them. Teachers also may be less willing to use a variety of instructional methods that will motivate and support students who are trying to learn. Teachers develop approaches that attempt to change African American students and parents so they will better fit into mainstream schools (King, 1994).

Cultural Difference Model

Teachers believe that the cause of underachievement in African American students stems from the cultural conflicts between home and school. Two of the profound cultural differences are in communication patterns and language dialect. The teacher may include more information about culture within the curriculum. Ultimately, this model also expects children to be resocialized, and minimal changes occur in the structure of schools (King, 1994).

Culturally Congruent and Centered Model

Teachers are seen as having key roles in the transformation of schools. The structure of schools is changed to reflect the knowledge, culture, and ways of knowing of African American students (King, 1994). Instructional strategies, curriculum, and policies are aimed at preparing African American students to become active participants in the creation of a more just society and reinforce the Black experience.

We believe teacher beliefs about the cause of the achievement gap of African American and mainstream students are relatively negative and fall into the first two categories of the culturally deficit and cultural difference models. We are concerned that these beliefs will effect the efficacy teachers hold about their abilities to reach African American students.

Teacher efficacy on student achievement is a crucial component of classroom effectiveness and refers to a teacher's belief about the power she or he has to produce an effect on students. Theoretically, the construct of efficacy arose from the social learning theory of Bandura (1986, 1989, 1991), who explored the notion of self-efficacy. The construct of teacher efficacy emerged in the research literature in the mid-1970s with the work from two studies funded by Title III and evaluated by the Rand Corporation (Armor et al., 1976; Berman, McLaughlin, Bass, Pauly, & Zellman, 1977). These two studies measured a sense of teacher efficacy using the total score on two Likert scale items: (a) When it comes right down to it, a teacher really can't do much because a student's motivation and performance depends on his or her home environment and (b) If I really try hard, I can get through to even the most difficult or unmotivated students.

Based on this work and the research of Gibson and Dembo (1984), Ashton and Webb (1986), and Woolfolk and Hoy (1990), the construct of teacher efficacy centers on two powerful dimensions, personal teaching efficacy and general teaching efficacy.

General teaching efficacy (TE) refers to an expectation about teaching and the power teachers believe they have to influence students. A teacher with low teaching efficacy tends to approach the teaching-learning process with the belief that some students will never achieve because of the influence of their home environment or socioeconomic status; there is little the teacher can do to overcome these factors because they are beyond his or her control.

The second dimension is personal teaching efficacy (PE), and it refers to personal competency or what a teacher believes about her or his own personal ability to produce an effect on students. This dimension refers to an individual's assessment of his or her own teaching competence. Teachers with high PE believe that all students can be motivated, and it is their responsibility to explore with students what tasks will hold their attention in the learning process.

The two dimensions allow researchers to examine how teachers feel generally about teaching and then to explore how an individual teacher feels about her or his abilities to reach students. We feel that this construct is extremely important because PE indicates how confident teachers feel about their own skills and abilities. Ashton and Webb (1986) used questionnaires, interviews, observations, and school documents and found low-efficacy teachers to be more critical and distrustful of students in comparison to high-efficacy teachers. Low-efficacy teachers continually needed to exert "control" over students. They were also less likely to use a variety of instructional strategies to reach low-achieving students. High-efficacy teachers created relatively harmonious classrooms and exhibited warm relationships with their students. They also provided more positive feedback to their students and felt responsible for the success of their students, regardless of their backgrounds. If teachers do not feel able to reach specific groups of students, then teachers will not have high expectations for the students, and they will also not work at providing a caring and culturally affirming classroom environment (Noddings, 1992).

Research has indicated that most teachers are middle-class European Americans and the majority of students from the 25 largest school districts in the United States are children of color who may be linguistically different and from low-income families (Banks, 1991). In addition, many teachers often have had limited contact with persons from underrepresented groups, and the experiential gap between teachers and their students may be large (Zeichner, 1993). Teachers have demonstrated uncomfortable feelings with racial and ethnic differences and perceived cultural diversity as an obstacle rather than a resource (Zeichner, 1993). For example, Dandy (1990) indicated that teachers have little knowledge of the cultural orientation of African American males, and teachers often misinterpret the behaviors of their students. Students may be highly verbal, using language to maintain identity, acquire status, and develop leadership within their community. This style of communication can be in direct conflict with classrooms where teachers are the primary speakers and students are expected to remain quiet and attentive to the teacher's words. Though this study does not look at specific aspects of African American cultural behavior, it does examine general beliefs about African American communities that are sources of cultural conflicts.

To examine both TE and PE as they relate to African American students, the following research questions were posed by this study:

1. When teacher efficacy survey items used in previous research studies are adapted to beliefs about African American students, do the results support the two-dimensional teacher efficacy construct of teaching efficacy and personal teaching efficacy that has been observed in earlier work?

2. Can teacher efficacy variables predict group membership between preservice and inservice teachers? What efficacy variables tend to be the best predictors of group membership?

3. Do significant differences exist between preservice and inservice teachers on the teacher efficacy survey instrument? Are inservice teachers more negative about their abilities to reach African American students?

4. What perceptions do preservice and inservice teachers have regarding their African American students and African American communities?

The Instrument

The instrument used to collect data on teacher beliefs about African American students was developed by adapting items from the work of Gibson and Dembo (1984),[1] Woolfolk and Hoy (1990), and Riggs and Enochs (1990). Thirty items were selected for the survey instrument. These items had consistent high-factor loadings across previous research studies or the item reflected an important aspect of teaching in relationship to African American students or both. The survey used a Likert scale to indicate agreement: strongly agree, agree, uncertain, disagree, and strongly disagree. In addition to the 30 survey items, 8 items were included to determine demographics, respondent's background, and experience with African American students and culture.

A principal axis factor analysis was conducted to demonstrate whether this adapted scale supported a two-dimensional construct of teacher efficacy: TE and PE. Two-tailed t tests were conducted and frequencies carefully reviewed.

Subjects

The survey was administered to 100 preservice and 75 inservice teachers who were enrolled in multicultural education courses during the spring of 1991 at a large Southern California university. The survey was given before the course work began.

Of the total 175 teachers, 129 or 74% were female, 41 or 23% were male, and 5 or 3% did not indicate their gender. Ethnic breakdown showed that 129 or 74% were European American, 24 or 13% were Latino-Hispanic, 10 or 6% were Asian Americans, 3 were African Americans, 4 were Native American, 1 was mixed-other, and 4 did not indicate their ethnicity.

When asked about teaching experience, 92 teachers or 53% had no teaching experience, 49 or 28% had between 1 and 5 years of teaching experience, 10 or 6% had between 6 and 9 years of teaching experience, and 24 teachers or 14% had 10 or more years with 7 teachers reporting experience between 20 and 31 years. Preservice teachers had an average teaching experience of 2.4 years; this was experience as a teacher aide or substitute. Inservice teachers had an average of 8.3 years of teaching experience. A total of 69 teachers had elementary teaching experience and 21 had experience teaching at the secondary level.

Among the 175 teachers, 120 teachers or 69% indicated that they had not taken any courses in multicultural education, 21 teachers or 12% indicated that they had taken at least one course, 17 teachers or 10% had taken two courses, and 17 teachers or 10% had taken three or more courses. One teacher indicated that she had taken nine courses in multicultural education.

■ Results

Personal and Teaching Efficacy Dimensions

The factor analysis indicated that the adapted teacher efficacy survey instrument supported the two-dimensional teacher efficacy construct of TE and PE that has been observed in earlier work. The two factors accounted for 26% of the variance. Factor 1 had an eigen value of 4.31 and accounted for 14.4 % of the variance. Factor 2 had an eigen value of 3.43 and accounted for 11.4 of the variance. The factor load of 70% of the items, 21 of the 30 items, loaded highest for factor 1 or 2. The results of the factor analysis for TE and PE can be found in Tables 3.1 and 3.2.

Differences Between Preservice and Inservice Teachers

The second research question focused on significant differences between preservice and inservice teachers on the teacher efficacy survey instrument. A discriminant function analysis was performed to deter-

TABLE 3.1   Factor Loadings and *t*-Test Results for Preservice and Inservice Teachers on Teaching Efficacy (TE) Items

Teaching Efficacy (TE) Item	Preservice Teachers		Inservice Teachers		Factor Loadings
	Mean	*SD*	*Mean*	*SD*	
16. A teacher is very limited in what he or she can achieve because an (African American's) home environment is a large influence on his or her achievement.	3.59	.83	3.56	.919	.67
14. If one of my new (African American) students cannot remain on task for a particular assignment, there is little that I could do to increase her or his attention until she or he is ready.	3.95	.642	3.94	.884	.63
2. The hours in my class have little influence on (African American) students compared to the influence of their home environment.	3.48	.95	3.63	.927	.57
17. Teachers are not a very powerful influence on (African American) student achievement when all factors are considered.	4.12	.656	3.84	.806*	.54
8. If (African American) students aren't disciplined at home, they aren't likely to accept any discipline.	3.40	.932	3.36	1.06	.52
25. If an African American student in my class becomes disruptive and noisy, I feel assured that I know some techniques to redirect him or her quickly.	2.49	.703	2.20	.753**	.52
11. Some (African American) students need to be placed in slower groups so that they are not subjected to unrealistic expectation.	3.86	.954	3.91	.111	.51
23. If (African American) parents would do more with their children, I could do more.	2.76	.933	2.51	.935	.38

*$p \le .05$; **$p \le .01$; ***$p \le .001$

TABLE 3.2   Factor Loadings and *t*-Test Results for Preservice and Inservice Teachers on Personal Efficacy (PE) Items

Personal Teaching Efficacy (PE) Item	Preservice Teachers		Inservice Teachers		Factor Loading
	Mean	SD	Mean	SD	
21. If an (African American) student masters a new math concept quickly, this might be because I knew the necessary steps in teaching the concept.	2.65	.957	2.44	.793	.60
19. When the grades of my (African American) student improve, it is usually because I found more effective teaching approaches.	2.55	.73	2.41	.718	.56
9. My teacher training program or experience or both has given me the necessary skills to be an effective teacher.	2.69	.734	2.24	.984***	.52
29. If one of my (African American) students couldn't do a class assignment, I would be able to accurately assess whether the assignment was the correct level of difficulty.	2.81	.677	2.35	.668***	.53
24. If an (African American) student did not remember information I gave in a previous lesson, I would know how to increase his or her retention in the next lesson.	2.85	.626	2.67	.844	.50
20. If my principal suggested that I change some of my class curriculum, I would feel confident that I have the necessary skills to implement the unfamiliar curriculum.	2.48	.745	1.99	.668***	.49
5. I have enough training to deal with almost any learning problem.	2.08	.800	2.71	.969***	.51

(continued)

TABLE 3.2 Continued

Personal Teaching Efficacy (PE) Item	Preservice Teachers		Inservice Teachers		Factor Loading
	Mean	SD	Mean	SD	
4. When an (African American) student gets a better grade than he or she usually gets, it is usually because I found better ways of teaching that student. (Higher load on Factor 2.)	2.72	.866	2.67	.875	.48
13. When an (African American) student is having difficulty with an assignment, I am usually able to adjust it to his or her level.	2.63	.734	2.31	.735**	.47
28. When an (African American) child progresses after being placed in a slower group, it is usually because the teacher has had a chance to give him or her extra attention. (Higher load on Factor 2.)	2.76	.780	2.69	.822	.47
3. If (African American) parents comment to me that their child behaves much better at school than he or she does home, it would probably be because I have some specific techniques of managing his or her behavior that they may lack.	2.74	1.03	2.827	1.02	.46
22. Parent conferences can help a teacher judge how much to expect from an (African American) student by giving the teacher an idea of the parent(s)' values toward education, discipline, and so forth.	2.39	1.07	2.45	.977	−.44
15. When I really try, I can get through to the most difficult (African American) student.	2.45	.783	2.28	.745	.35

**$p \leq .01$; ***$p \leq .001$

TABLE 3.3 Personal Efficacy and Teaching Efficacy Means and Standard Deviations for Preservice and Inservice Teachers

Variable	Preservice		Inservice	
	Mean	*SD*	*Mean*	*SD*
Personal efficacy	30.99	4.41	28.08	4.91***
Teaching efficacy	27.92	3.29	27.20	3.74

***$p \leq .001$

mine if beliefs statements could discriminate between preservice and inservice teachers. The analysis resulted in a significance level .01 with an eigen value of .351 and Wilks Lambda of .739. The discriminant function was able to correctly group 128 of 175 cases or 73.1% of the teachers in the group. Five variables emerged in the structure coefficients that were significant in the resulting discriminant function, four in the PE category (Items 5, 9, 20, and 29) and one in the TE category, Item 25.

The third question looked at survey differences between preservice and inservice teachers. Preservice teachers were found to demonstrate significantly higher scores on the PE dimension of the construct than inservice teachers. There was no difference on their TE dimensions. These results can be found in Table 3.3.

Preservice teachers had significantly higher efficacy scores on the following questions:

- 17. Teachers are not a very powerful influence on African American student achievement when all factors are considered. (A high-efficacy teacher would strongly disagree with this statement.)

- 19. If one of my African American students couldn't do a class assignment, I would be able to accurately assess whether the assignment was the correct level of difficulty.

- 25. If an African American student in my class becomes disruptive and noisy, I feel assured that I know some techniques to redirect him or her quickly.

- 13. When an African American student is having difficulty with an assignment, I am usually able to adjust it to his or her level.

Preservice and inservice teachers also did not show any differences on a number of items. The frequencies for the following items demonstrate positive, neutral, or negative feelings about African American communities.

- 2. The hours in my class have little influence on African American students compared to the influence of their home environment.

  As a group, 59% of the teachers strongly disagreed or disagreed, whereas 41% were uncertain, agreed, or strongly agreed.

- 8. If African American students aren't disciplined at home, they aren't likely to accept any discipline.

  Taken as a group, 56% strongly disagreed or disagreed, whereas 44% were neutral, agreed, or strongly agreed.

- 16. A teacher is very limited in what he or she can achieve because an African American's home environment is a large influence on his or her environment.

  Taken as a group, 66% strongly disagreed or disagreed, whereas 34% were uncertain, agreed, or strongly agreed.

- 30. Even a teacher with good teaching abilities may not reach many African American students.

  Taken as a group, 35% disagreed, whereas 65% were uncertain, agreed, or strongly agreed.

- 24. If an African American student did not remember information I gave in a previous lesson, I would know how to increase his or her retention in the next lesson.

  Taken as a group, 36% strongly agreed or agreed, whereas 54% were uncertain or disagreed.

- 15. When I really try, I can get through to the most difficult African American student.

  Taken as a group 63% strongly agreed or agreed, whereas 37% were uncertain, disagreed, or strongly disagreed.

Some responses indicate that teachers do feel they can make a difference in the lives of their African American students.

- 17. Teachers are not a very powerful influence on African American student achievement when all factors are considered.

  Taken as a group, 83% strongly disagreed or disagreed, whereas only 17% were uncertain, agreed, or strongly agreed.

- 11. Some African American students need to be placed in slower groups so that they are not subjected to unrealistic expectations.

  Taken as a group, 73% strongly disagreed or disagreed, whereas 27% were uncertain, agreed, or strongly agreed.

■ Cultural Familiarity of Teachers

Familiarity with African Americans and the African American culture was divided. The survey showed that 47% ($n = 82$) felt they knew a lot about African American culture and values, 29% ($n = 50$) indicated that they did not know a lot about African American culture, and 24% ($n = 43$) were uncertain. When asked if they had many African American friends, the results were again divided: 46% ($n = 81$) of the teachers indicated that they did have many African American friends, 45% ($n = 78$) said they did not, and 9% ($n = 16$) were uncertain. When asked if they had gone to a school where there were African American students, the majority of the teachers, 70% ($n = 122$), indicated they had not; 28% ($n = 49$) indicated that they had; and 2% ($n = 4$) were uncertain that they had gone to a school with African American students. When asked it they felt they had grown up in a household where there was racism, the majority of the teachers, 71% ($n = 124$), indicated that they felt they had not, whereas 21% ($n = 36$) said they did, and 9% ($n = 15$) were uncertain.

Implications

We found racial attitudes did affect teacher efficacy beliefs of preservice and inservice teachers in our sample. Their responses demonstrated how racial attitudes need to be examined when looking at teacher expectations, confidence, and beliefs about teaching. There were four main findings.

First, our study replicated the existence of a two-dimensional construct of teacher efficacy when the statements in the survey included the term *African American*. We believe the PE and TE dimensions can bring to light how teacher attitudes toward students from underrepresented groups may affect student achievement. This study indicates that teacher efficacy, particularly PE, can discriminate between the seasoned and novice teacher.

The second finding indicated that our predominately European American sample had a limited knowledge of African American students and culture. Less then half of the teachers indicated they knew much about African American culture or had many African American friends. In addition, almost three quarters of the sample did not go to school with African Americans. The fact that 69% had not taken any multicultural education courses gives evidence that many teachers have little, if any, formal training in understanding what education has meant, can mean, and will continue to mean to African American students.

The question that we raise is, Where do teachers acquire information about African American children? If they did not have experiences growing up and they do not take multicultural education courses that will advance their knowledge of African American culture and values, how then are teacher beliefs formed? Can teachers change their attitudes about schooling of underrepresented students if they do not fully understand the scope and dynamics of the youngsters they are hoping to teach? Are teacher beliefs and opinions about African Americans primarily formed through vicarious experiences, such as what they read, hear, and see on television, radio, and the newspapers? If this is true, it is more than likely that certification programs, inservice teacher training programs, and college courses have painfully neglected a vital component in their preparatory and inservice programs. Though many teacher education courses are found at the end of a preservice student's college experience, the inclusion of African American history, culture, behavioral patterns, economic opportunities, and literature should be addressed throughout a college education. If teachers have few opportunities to build relationships with or learn about African American traditions and value orientations, teachers may not have the chance to examine the stereotypical beliefs they may hold. Furthermore, teachers are aware of the limitations of their training. Marshall (1991) found that teachers had concerns about their own professional abilities, particularly their content knowledge about culturally diverse students. The majority of the teachers from this survey believed that their teacher training programs did not provide them with necessary skills to be effective teachers.

The third finding indicates that preservice teachers are more positive about their ability to reach African American children than inservice teachers. They indicated more ability to assess, redirect, teach, and adjust to the needs of African American students. The responses of seasoned teachers may show that their ability to make changes in students are limited to factors beyond their control (i.e., poverty, dysfunctional parents, lack of teaching materials, and large class sizes). Seasoned teachers may have been influenced over a period of time by others who have not been able to address the needs of African American students. If teachers at a school are voicing predominantly negative perceptions about African American students, then as problems arise, new teachers may learn to use cultural conflict and lack of knowledge about African American students as scapegoats for scholastic failure. Because preservice teachers demonstrated significantly more efficacy, then we believe socialization of new teachers by the system is so strong that they come to emulate negative feelings about African American students that they find in their more experienced colleagues.

The most troubling finding of this study was the large number of teachers who did not feel they could effectively teach African American students. Forty-one percent did not disagree with a statement that indicated that their class had little influence on African American students when compared to the influence of their homes; 65% did not disagree with the statement that even a teacher with good teaching abilities may not reach African American youth. A strong underlying belief seems to prevail that the African American community is not supportive of education.

Teacher efficacy is a complicated construct. An overwhelming percentage, 83%, disagreed with the statement that teachers are not a very powerful influence on African American student achievement when all factors are considered. However, as stated earlier, teachers did indicate ambivalence in reaching some African American students. The findings point to the belief that though teachers are generally effective with students, there are those students whom no one would be able to reach. In addition, 73% of the teachers did not believe in putting African American students in lower ability groups. This response demonstrated that teachers did not believe in tracking or ability grouping based on racial membership.

Responses to survey statements seemed to indicate that teachers had mixed feelings about teaching African American students. Generally, the teachers in our sample did not feel confident about their personal abilities to teach African American children. Teachers may be saying that the failure of African American students to achieve is not a teacher failure. Teacher responses demonstrated that they believed a lack of discipline from the home, negligence of parents, and low student interest are the main reasons why a gap between African American children and European American children exists in school achievement. The teachers in our study seemed to endorse the cultural-deficit view of learning. Lightfoot (1978) believed teachers do not understand that the behavior of African American parents and students may reflect a frustration with schools rather than an uncaring attitude toward learning.

> The literature shows overwhelmingly that blacks[sic] (regardless of social status) universally view education as the most promising means for attaining higher socioeconomic status. The dissonance between black parents and teachers, therefore, does not lie in the conflicting values attached to education but in the misconceptions they have of one another.
>
> Despite the passionate and often unrealistic dreams of black parents, teachers continue to view them as uncaring, sympathetic, and ignorant of the value of education for their children. . . . Often they perceive the parents' lack of involvement in ritualistic school events and parent conferences as apathy and disinterest and rarely interpret it as the inability to negotiate the bureaucratic maze of schools or as a response to a long history of exclusion and rejection at the school door. (Lightfoot, 1978, p. 166)

■ Conclusion

Teacher efficacy is an important construct in student achievement, and teacher educators need to seriously examine what teachers believe about their abilities to teach children from various underrepresented groups, particularly African American students. Stereotypical notions about specific ethnic groups are powerful perceptions, and teacher training institutions must address the issues of race, ethnicity, and culture throughout their certification programs (Grant, 1995; Nieto, Young, Tran, & Pang, 1994; Sleeter & Grant, 1994; Zeichner, 1993). Inservice development must include opportunities for teachers to examine how their belief systems influence what they do and how they teach children from various nonmainstream ethnic groups; otherwise, negative beliefs may be reinforced (Goodwin, 1994; Haberman, 1991). In addition, teacher education programs should focus more attention on issues of teacher-student relationships (Noddings, 1992; Pang, 1994). How can a teacher create a trusting and motivating environment? Which incidents are rooted in cultural conflict? When the overwhelming majority of the teaching force in this country has experiences that differ from their students, the need to look at teacher misconceptions of African Americans' culture, customs, history, and values is essential.

The impact of other racial and ethnic attitudes on teacher efficacy may be subtle and also needs to be addressed in teacher education programs. How do teachers feel about Mexican American students or Chinese American students? Do teachers believe, for example, that children who speak Vietnamese or Spanish may be hampered in their cognitive growth? Are there differences in teacher expectations and teaching efficacy depending on the ethnic group?

Teacher educators must work tirelessly to facilitate the development of high-efficacy teachers (Ashton & Webb, 1986). Teachers must be moved away from using race or socioeconomic background as excuses for the nonperformance of their students. Hale-Benson (1989) and Irvine (1990) believed mainstream teachers and African American students may experience cultural conflict. Successful teachers realize African American students have a distinctively different cultural background and create educational programs that motivate and interest students. The teachers who are effective with African American students develop strong bonds, have high expectations, focus on the total child, and use familiar communications styles (Foster, 1994).

Schooling can be a liberatory experience for African American students (Ladson-Billings, 1992). High-efficacy teachers use methodologies that are meaningful to students and integrate the spoken and cultural traditions of African Americans into their classrooms. For example, African American students can be encouraged to be leaders in class discussions and ask complex questions. In addition, teachers can openly discuss the negative portrayals of African Americans in the media, focusing dialogue on accurate portrayals. Students learn about society's hidden curriculum (Foster, 1994). Teachers may choose literature that challenges the inequalities students find in their lives. When students have the chance to question and delve into social issues, the curriculum no longer rests on a culturally deficit model; rather, schooling becomes relevant and transformative (King, 1994).

Ladson-Billings (1992) found successful teachers of African American children to have a strong sense of purpose. They were committed to facilitating the growth of their students. They also understood the sociopolitical experience of African Americans in U.S. society and believed in preparing students to deal with social inequities. In addition, the teachers were confident about their abilities and developed caring and trusting relationships with their students. We urge teacher educators to direct preservice and inservice teachers not only to examine their beliefs about African American students, but to facilitate an investigation into how their beliefs may serve as obstacles to the creation of warm, challenging, and successful classrooms for children.

■ Note

1. Material from Gibson and Dembo (1984) was used with permission of the authors.

■ References

Armor, D., Conry-Oseguera, P., Cox, M., King, N., McDonnell, L., Pascal, A., Pauly, E., & Zellman, G. (1976). *Analysis of the school preferred reading program in selected Los Angeles minority schools* (Report No. R-2007-LAUSD). Santa Monica, CA: RAND. (ERIC Document Reproduction Service No. ED 130 243)

Ashton, P. T., & Webb, R. B. (1986). *Making a difference: Teachers' sense of efficacy and student achievement* (Research on Teaching monograph series). New York: Longman.

Ashton, P., Webb, R., & Doda, N. (1983). *A study of teachers' sense of efficacy* (Final Report, National Institute of Education Contract Mp/ 400-79-0075). Gainesville: University of Florida. (ERIC Document Reproduction Service No. ED 231-834)

Bandura, A. (1986). *Social foundations of thought and action: A social cognitive theory.* Englewood Cliffs, NJ: Prentice Hall.

Bandura, A. (1989). Human agency in social cognitive theory. *American Psychologist, 77,* 122-147.

Bandura, A. (1991). Self-regulation of motivation through anticipatory and self reactive mechanisms. In R. A. Dienstbier (Ed.), *Perspectives on motivation: Nebraska symposium on motivation* (Vol. 38, pp 69-164). Lincoln: University of Nebraska Press.

Banks, J. A. (1991). Teaching multicultural literacy to teachers. *Teaching Education, 4*(1), 135-144.

Banks, J. A., & Banks, C. M. (Eds.). (1995). *Handbook of research on multicultural education.* New York: Macmillan.

Berman, P., McLaughlin, M., Bass, G., Pauly, E., & Zellman, G. (1977). *Federal programs supporting educational change. Vol. 7: Factors affecting implementation and continuation.* Santa Monica, CA: RAND. (ERIC Document Reproduction Service No. ED 140 432)

Bowie, R., & Bond, C. (1994). Influencing future teachers' attitudes toward Black English: Are we making a difference? *Journal of Teacher Education, 45*(2), 112-118.

Dandy, E. B. (1990). *Sensitizing teachers to cultural differences: An African American perspective.* Paper presented at the National Dropout Prevention Conference, Tennessee. (ERIC Document Reproduction Service No. ED 323 479)

Ford, D. Y. (1992). The American achievement ideology and achievement differentials among preadolescent gifted and nongifted African American males and females. *Journal of Negro Education, 61*(1), 45-64.

Foster, M. (1994). Effective Black teachers: A literature review. In E. Hollins, J. King, & W. Hayman (Eds.), *Teaching diverse populations: Formulating a knowledge base* (pp. 225-242). Albany: State University of New York Press.

Gibson, S., & Dembo, M. H. (1984). Teacher efficacy: A construct validation. *Journal of Educational Psychology, 76*(4), 569-582.

Goodwin, A. L. (1994). Making the transition from self to other: What do pre-service teachers really think about multicultural education? *Journal of Teacher Education, 45*(2), 119-131.

Grant, C. (1995, November). *Critical knowledge, skills, and experiences for the introduction of culturally diverse students: A perspective for the preparation of preservice teachers.* Paper presented at the Center for Urban Learning/Teaching and Urban Research in Education and Schools, Atlanta, GA.

Haberman, M. (1991). The rationale for training adults as teachers. In C. E. Sleeter (Ed.), *Empowerment through multicultural education* (pp. 275-286). Albany: State University of New York Press.

Hale-Benson, J. (1989). The school learning environment and academic success. In G. Berry & J. Asamen (Eds.), *Black students' psychosocial issues and academic achievement* (pp. 83-97). Newbury Park, CA: Sage.

Irvine, J. J. (1990). *Black students and school failure.* New York: Greenwood.

Jenkins, L. (1989). The Black family and academic achievement. In G. Berry & J. Asamen (Eds.), *Black students' psychosocial issues and academic achievement* (pp. 138-152). Newbury Park, CA: Sage.

King, J. (1994). The purpose of schooling for African American children: Including cultural knowledge. In E. Hollins, J. King, & Warren Hayman (Eds.), *Teaching diverse populations: Formulating a knowledge base* (pp. 25-60). Albany: State University of New York Press.

Ladson-Billings, G. (1992). Liberatory consequences of literacy: A case of culturally relevant instruction for African American students. *Journal of Negro Education, 61*(3), 378-391.

Lightfoot, S. (1978). *Worlds apart: Relationships between families and schools.* New York: Basic Books.

Lomotey, K. (Ed.). (1990). *Going to school: The African American experience.* New York: State University of New York Press.

Marshall, P. L. (1991, November). *Juxtaposing Steele's thesis on the African American student and pre-service education majors' concerns about teaching diverse students*. Paper presented at the National Council for the Social Studies Annual Meeting in Washington, DC. (ERIC Document Reproduction Service No. ED 339 285)

Nieto, J., Young, R., Tran, M., & Pang, V. O. (1994). Passionate commitment to a multicultural society: Coming of age in teacher education. *Equity and Excellence in Education, 27*(1), 51-57.

Noddings, N. (1992). *The challenge to care*. New York: Teachers College Press.

Pang, V. (1988). Ethnic prejudice: Still alive and hurtful. *Harvard Educational Review, 58*(3), 375-379.

Pang, V. (1994). Why do we need *this* class? Multicultural education for teachers. *Phi Delta Kappan, 76*(4), 289-292.

Poplin, M. (1992). Educating in diversity. *Executive Educator, 14*(3), A18-A24.

Riggs, I. M., & Enochs, L. G. (1990). Toward the development of an elementary teacher's science teaching efficacy belief instrument. *Science Education, 74*(6), 625-637.

Rubovitz, P., & Maehr, M. (1973). Pygmalion Black and White. *Journal of Personality and Social Psychology, 25*(2), 210-218.

Sleeter, C., & Grant, C. (1994). *Making choices for multicultural education* (2nd ed.). New York: Macmillan.

Tran, M., Young, R., & DiLella, J. (1994). Multicultural education courses and the student teacher: Eliminating stereotypical attitudes in our ethnically diverse classroom. *Journal of Teacher Education, 45*(3), 183-189.

Villegas, A. M. (1991). *Culturally responsive pedagogy for the 1990s and beyond* (Trends and Issues Paper No. 6). Washington, DC: ERIC Clearinghouse on Teacher Education, American Association of Colleges For Teacher Education.

Woolfolk, A. E., & Hoy, W. K (1990). Prospective teacher's sense of efficacy and beliefs about control. *Journal of Educational Psychology, 82*(1), 81-91.

Zeichner, K. (1993). *Educating teachers for cultural diversity*. East Lansing, MI: National Center for Research on Teacher Learning.

PART II

Culture

A View Toward the Unexplored Frontier

■ *Michael Webb*

> *Culture is to humans as water is to fish.*
>
> —WADE A. NOBLES, May 1994

This chapter will present one argument for the inclusion of African and African American culture as part of professional development. Certainly, teachers and other educators of African American students benefit from knowledge and appreciation of the students' culture. In this context, Carter G. Woodson (1933) advised teachers to discover their students' background as a way to explore their responsibilities.

More than 60 years after Carter G. Woodson wrote these words, his advice for the most part remains unheeded. Professional development, whether preservice or inservice, is not designed to help educators find answers to such questions as, "How can we assess the curriculum to insure that it reflects the culture, experiences and contributions of Africans and African Americans?" "How do my own attitudes about the potential of African American students influence my personal teaching style and classroom behavior?" "In what ways can the learner's frame of reference help him or her in learning and applying new content?" "What do we know about African and African American culture that can be used to inspire and empower students to achieve greater academic success?" The current crisis in public education warrants our best efforts to help educators to seek and find answers to these important questions.

Although there are numerous examples of African American students who have attained high levels of academic achievement, the inability of the public schools to meet the educational needs of large numbers of African American students has led some observers to question whether cultural biases in the curriculum or in teaching practice might be at least partially responsible for the problem. Current approaches to teaching and learning have left a disproportionate percentage of African American students ill-prepared to achieve personal success in postsecondary education or employment or both and to assume roles as meaningful contributors to their community and to society as a whole.

Today, in public forums and on the pages of scientific and popular journals, educators, researchers, and others grapple with the extent to which African and African American culture should be reflected in curricula and pedagogy. The discussions are often clouded by misconceptions regarding the meaning of "culture." For example, the term is sometimes used to describe socioeconomic status or practices that actually constitute listings of significant historical events; biographies of figures of note; or information pertaining to food, music, and dress.

All of these reflect important aspects of culture; however, culture more appropriately refers to a shared pattern of institutions, behaviors, traditions, values, and beliefs. Culture is not static. It adapts to collective experiences and to changing societal conditions. Culture is "lived and learned every day through the way family members interact, through language, family stories, family values, and spiritual life; through household customs and the work family members do" (Derman-Sparks, 1995, p. 17). In essence, culture is a shared design for living.

Professional development should train educators to place students and their cultures at the center of learning, to acknowledge, respect, and build on the knowledge, beliefs, and experiences that students bring with them to the classroom and to affirm rather than negate the value of students' cultures. Professional development should also prepare educators to counter the omissions, misconceptions, and distortions regarding the vital contributions of Africans and African Americans to the story of humanity.

*Throughout America today we are given repeatedly the dismal report
and picture of underachievement and underrepresentation of African,
Native and Latino Americans: in the mathematical sciences, engineer-
ing and technology. In terms of historical time this is a recent phenome-
non. At least up until the fall of Granada in Spain in 1492 C.E., the
year that Columbus [arrived in this hemisphere], African, Native and
Latino Americans in their ancestors were the leaders of all intellectual
pursuits in the arts and sciences.* (Shabazz, n.d.)

■ Culture and Education

Considerations of the role of African and African American culture in
teaching and learning focus on two overlapping needs: (a) the need to
address the effects of racism and ethnocentrism and (b) the need to make
the curriculum reflect the diverse experiences of African Americans.

Racism and Ethnocentrism

Education should affirm the inherent value of each student and the
centrality of his or her experiences. When schools disaffirm the culture
of African Americans, whether explicitly or implicitly, they send a subtle
message that "who you are and what you know are of little value."

In the United States and Europe, the legacy of systematic attempts to
dehumanize Africans and African Americans, over more than three cen-
turies, is an enduring human tragedy. Persistent claims of African
American inferiority and low expectations regarding the learning potential of African American students are outcomes of the tragedy.

Textbooks, media, and "scholarly" publications continue to perpetuate the myth of European racial and cultural superiority. The omission
of the contributions of Africans and African Americans from the curriculum in all disciplines reinforces the misconception that they have offered
little to world civilization.

Yet in the long annals of civilization, the denigration of Africa and
people of African descent is but a recent affair:

With the collapse of Songhay in 1594 C.E., the entire western region
of Africa was left unprotected. Only small kingdoms with weak ar-
mies remained to defend the vast coastal borders. This made it easy
for the European nations to occupy some sections of the African

coast. One hundred years after the first European invasion in 1441 C.E., Africans would be found in every part of the Western Hemisphere as indentured servants or enslaved people. So profitable and valuable would Africans become to European entrepreneurs, whose main concern was making money, that the enslavement of Africans would become one of the keys to industrializing Europe and America. (Asante, 1995, p. 10)

An accurate understanding of history is necessary to help the nation overcome the social afflictions, created by racism and ethnocentrism, that threaten the very fabric of our society.

Reflecting African Americans in the Curriculum

The story of African Americans begins in Africa and continues in the Americas. African Americans have influenced almost every major social, political, and economic change within the United States.

Understanding the conditions and quality of African American life requires an understanding of the influences of major historical events that occurred before and after the arrival in significant numbers of Africans on this continent.

African and African American culture represent a central, though too often neglected, chapter in the historical and contemporary chronicle of humanity's social, political, and economic evolution. Professional preparation for teachers and other educators should include learning about the important role that Africa has played throughout world history, how African social institutions were destroyed during the period of European enslavement, the resistance of African people to colonialism and enslavement, and the experiences of African people in the Americas and the Caribbean.

African American intellect and creativity have enriched the quality of life within the United States and the world.

The profoundly diverse cultural heritage of African Americans has placed it in its proper perspective of a people's history that is holistic, comprehensive and thematic . . . the history of peoples of African descent is richly intertwined with that of the cultures of the world whether they be in the Americas, north or south, the Caribbean, Europe, Asia or the Pacific Isles. (Thompson, 1990, p. 68)

Knowledge of the experiences and contributions of Africans and African Americans in every discipline and historical period is not only of importance to educators working with African American students. The inclusion of such knowledge is essential in order to provide all students with an education that reflects the principles of honesty, academic integrity, thoroughness, and accuracy.

> *Approaches emphasizing remediation and/or treatment of "risk" may appear to work for some students, but these interventions have failed to contribute in a substantial way to academic excellence overall. Notions of student deprivation and risk are philosophically at odds with the conviction that "all children can and will learn."* (Commission on Students of African Descent, 1996, p. 1)

Culture and Expectations

Asa Hilliard (1995) has observed that, "We have embraced a prediction paradigm that tells us that students are gifted, average, or retarded" (p. 4). Teachers form opinions about the academic abilities of black students regardless of their actual academic potential (Gay & Gilbert, 1985).

A teacher's judgment of a student's potential results in expectations for achievement that

> are communicated both overtly and implicitly. The best example of overt communication is the process of tracking students based upon the perceptions teachers have of individual students. The student, in turn, translates these teacher-based expectations into either positive or negative outcomes related to achievement, aspiration, and self-concept. (Ploumis-Devick & Follman, 1993, p. 9)

It is no wonder that so many of our children live down to our low expectations of them. Children are capable of recognizing unfocused, half-hearted instruction and are capable of responding with efforts equally unfocused and half-hearted.

In fact, educational practices actually perpetuate the lack of academic success of African American students. For example, often, the least qualified teachers are assigned to schools with a majority of African American students. Disproportionate numbers of African American students are trapped in the less demanding academic tracks and general education. These practices provide stark measures of what schools expect that African American students can achieve.

African American students are also characterized in ways that communicate clearly a lack of belief in their abilities and potential, for example, at-risk, disadvantaged, culturally deprived (the *Education Index* cross-references "Black Students" with the phrase "culturally deprived").

But how is it possible that the same children who do not succeed in some classrooms succeed quite well in others? It is clear that challenging academic content, parent or family involvement, and high expectations help to explain why some educators and entire schools have experienced tremendous success.

Expectations—both those we hold for children and those they hold for themselves—exert a powerful influence on children's level of effort and sense of personal efficacy. It is argued here that low expectations of African American students derive from misconceptions about learning ability, stereotypes perpetuated by social institutions (including schools), and lack of understanding of and appreciation for students' cultures and experiences.

There is ample evidence that all students can indeed achieve. Research studies and anecdotes of successful teachers illustrate that learners from all backgrounds are capable of performing and achieving at significantly higher levels than they normally achieve (Adler, 1984; Cohen, 1993; Comer, 1988; Levin, 1990; Matthews, 1988; Slavin, 1994). Underachieving students can indeed change and perform as high achievers.

Lack of achievement is a condition that can be addressed, and not an end result. However, policy makers, educators, and others are faced with the dilemma of how to overcome intractable attitudes about student potential in order to convert these principles into practical working programs, including professional development, for all public schools and particularly schools serving large concentrations of African American students.

> *African American history is a story that begins in Africa and continues in the Americas. In this country, it is a documentation of the life experiences of African people within the United States and should be interpreted in reference to the cultural interchange that has had a mutual influence on both the African culture within the United States and other cultural expression throughout this society.* (Hollins & Nobles, 1993, p. 15)

Culture and Learning Style

Differences in societal and personal experiences are reflected in the tremendous diversity among African Americans. However, the majority of African Americans, and particularly those who grow up in segregated African American environments, share aspects of a common culture grounded in history, values, language, and experience, including the experience of racism and discrimination. This shared culture holds several implications for learning style.

However, the discussion of culture and learning style must not be used as a smokescreen to mask low expectations regarding what African American students are capable of achieving. To achieve personal and economic success in our society, all students must develop character and discipline; they must assume responsibility for themselves as lifelong learners.

Schools must help students to cultivate the skills and competencies they need for success in school and beyond. Where instructional methods and strategies are ineffective, it is the role of the schools to identify and use alternative approaches based on an assessment of student culture, needs, and learning style.

Researchers who have focused on African American culture have identified broad generalizations as well as implications for teaching and learning. Although considerations of culture alone may not adequately explain why some African American students excel in the same environment in which so many others do not, an emerging body of work provides clues regarding the influences of culture on learning and learning styles. An overview of findings of research on African American social practices, compiled by Hollins and Nobles (1993), is presented in Table 4.1.

A growing body of research explores the implications of African American culture for teaching and learning (Guild, 1994; Hale, 1982; Hilliard, 1995; Ladson-Billings, 1994; Nobles & Mann, 1995; Pasteur & Toldson, 1982). This research, summarized by Jackson (1990), indicates that many African American learners are apt to prefer lessons that establish relationships among concepts and express dissatisfaction with the memorization of discrete, unconnected "facts."

In the classroom, many students are easily distracted during long periods of sedentary, static, and solitary activities. They prefer animated instructional activities where planned, purposeful movement is a part of the learning activity. They also prefer feeling or emotion-based instruc-

TABLE 4.1   Generalizations About African American Social Practices

- The traditional African American family is composed of several individual households with the family definition and lines of authority and support transcending or going beyond any one single household unit.
- Structurally, the African American family expands and diminishes in response to external societal conditions.
- The African American family is child centered and finds its raison d'etre in the presence and development of children.
- The African American family is often characterized by close networks of relationships between families who may not necessarily be related by blood.
- In African American families, role definitions and role performance can be flexible and interchangeable. However, role definitions are always strictly sex linked, whereas role performance is sexless.
- Values within the African American community are shaped by and derived from two primary influences: (a) creative responses to racism and oppression and (b) carry-overs or retention of African traditions and beliefs.
- The African American family as an institution, regardless of class status, has to constantly struggle against racism, prejudice, discrimination, and cultural conflict and although being diverse economically, politically, and socially, they all are bicultural.
- There are cultural values or practices shared by African American communities regardless of socioeconomic status.
- African American families frequently participate in extensive kinship networks (derived from African origins), which serve as major emotional, economic, and social support.
- Urban African American families have developed adaptive strategies, resourcefulness, and resilience under conditions of perpetual poverty.
- Socially valued behaviors within the African American community include the spontaneous expression of emotions, public performance, personal style, compassion, race loyalty, and adaptability.
- Values orientation in African American communities tends to be communal, emotional, person centered, and flexible.
- African American parents prepare their children for the society as they have experienced it.

TABLE 4.1 Continued

- Important aspects of child-rearing practices include extended family participation, person-centeredness, early autonomy, and strong peer relationships among adolescents.
- Within the African American family, females are generally included in decision making; there is open acceptance of human sexuality, a minimum of sex role stereotyping in child rearing and parenting, and acceptance of unwed mothers and single parents.
- The relationship within families tends to be cooperative and egalitarian.
- Extended kinspeople take an active role in child rearing.
- Families set high expectations for their children's achievement within the society.
- Religion has been a strong and important force in validating and sustaining African American culture.

SOURCE: *Understanding African American Culture: A Teacher's Guide* (Nobles, 1994).

tional presentations or activities where the presenter is obviously involved in the subject or activity.

Students cooperate out of a sense of loyalty, personal affinity, and feelings; they are highly empathetic and respond positively to frequent constructive feedback or correct information provided to an incorrect response in a kind manner. They are sensitive to how the teacher feels about or perceives the student.

Contrast these generalizations about the culture and preferred learning styles of many African American students to traditional methods of instruction. Often, instructional methods work best for hard-to-distract students, who are able to concentrate and work long periods of time on assigned work.

For example, in most classrooms, students must adapt to the teacher's methods and instructional strategies, regardless of personal characteristics, such as exhibited learning style. Ultimately, students either "get it" (and succeed) or don't get it (and fail).

The teacher's orientation is to place a greater emphasis on whether or not a student got it than on "how can I make sure that he or she gets it." Nowhere is this dichotomy more evident than in classes for so-called gifted students in which multiple paths to discovery and learning are expected and encouraged.

Jackson (1990) also discusses characteristics of what she refers to as "low-yield" (in terms of student outcomes) teaching methods in working with many African American students.

Individuals who possess a low-yield teaching style prefer emotionally uninvolved, controlled, impersonal, matter-of-fact presentations or activities. They usually do not encourage or accept students' feelings as legitimate responses. They believe it is relatively unimportant how they "feel about" students as long as they do their job.

They give feedback primarily by marking what is wrong on papers submitted and graded. They often do not react or comment after students' oral responses. They emphasize subject-centered curricula or activities based on a perception of what students need to know, with little attempt to communicate why to the students or to assess students' prior knowledge or readiness to learn.

They assume automatic transfer by students—of the knowledge, skills, and information presented—to new situations. They are geared toward unanimated instructional activities where students are able to complete assignments independently, primarily through reading and writing.

The culture of many African Americans often places them at odds with the school. African American children are penalized frequently for failing to conform to teacher norms. As Herbert Foster (1986) illustrates, the inability of many teachers to recognize and respond to subtle cultural cues far too often results in inappropriate decisions, including unnecessary confrontations and referrals to disciplinary action or Special Education. Students who are not performing well in school often face a situation in which they must "sink or swim."

The rigid order and strict scheduling of activities contrasts sharply with what we know about learning styles in general. The lack of convergence between pedagogy, school structure and curriculum, and preferred learning style is an issue that must be addressed through professional development.

However, the majority of teachers of African American children complete their preservice training with little or no attention to the culture of African Americans or how this culture may influence ways in which students respond to different instructional approaches. Rarely explored is how culture may present opportunities for teaching and learning.

Among other things, excellence in education must prepare a student for self-knowledge and to become a contributing problem-solving member of his or her own community and in the wider world as well. No child can be ignorant of or lack respect for his or her own unique cultural group and meet others in the world on an equal footing. (National Alliance of Black School Educators, Inc., Task Force on Black Academic and Cultural Excellence, 1984, p. 11)

Implications for Professional Development

Most educators who work with African American students have not been adequately prepared to take advantage of the opportunities presented by these students' culture or to face the challenges they encounter in the school. Teachers are most often unfamiliar with the communities from which their students come and experience difficulty in communicating with students and their parents and families. According to an annual survey (Harris & Associates, 1992), teachers at schools with high concentrations of students of color are much more likely than others to cite lack of parental and school administration support and social problems as reasons for leaving the profession.

Consider that most teachers of African American children complete their professional development courses without benefit of any examination of the institutions, cultural traits, behaviors, values, and attitudes that African American students bring to the classroom. They are unfamiliar with strategies for incorporating information related to African and African American culture in every discipline and for using the information as motivational and inspirational stimuli to influence African American students to continue and expand their level of achievement.

Often, the college training of new teachers has not prepared them for social and cultural variables they encounter in the classroom. Most new teachers are unprepared to face the challenge of student underachievement, particularly in mathematics and science.

Characteristics of Successful Educators

Gloria Ladson-Billings (1994) presents case studies of successful teachers of African American children. What these teachers all had in common was that they consistently demonstrated their belief that all students can succeed. They were knowledgeable and competent in their subject areas. They possessed an understanding that high expectations and respect for the student are key and that both teaching approaches and content have to fit the students, and not the other way around.

Furthermore, these teachers viewed themselves as members of the community and saw teaching as a way of giving back to the community and encouraging their students to do the same. They helped students make connections between their community and the broader global society. They considered teaching to be an art and their role to dig knowledge out of students. They also recognized that by listening and learning from the students, they would often need to rethink and reenvision their instructional approach (Ladson-Billings, 1994).

> *City by city, school by school, classroom by classroom, child by child, things can be done. The situation can seem overwhelmingly hopeless if we do nothing but take the long, dismal view.* (Cartwright & D'Orso, 1993, p. 225)

A New Vision for Professional Development

Despite the challenges we face today, we are fortunate to have access to a rich and growing knowledge base of models, strategies, and approaches that have been effective in educating African American children. Increasingly, education and reform initiatives call for contextualization of learning in everyday life, drawing on the learner's experience, hands-on learning, and valuing what the student brings to the classroom.

One of the major tasks before us is to bring the system of professional development into congruence with what has been learned. Institutions of higher education and school and district professional development programs must be restructured to provide educators with the skills and knowledge they need to address the challenges.

Schools, Colleges, and Departments of Education

These have a leading role to play in restructuring professional development. In addition to requiring competence in a specific discipline or subject area, they can ensure that educators are knowledgeable about African and African American history and culture. The required course of study should include African and African American history. Courses should develop educators' abilities to incorporate material on African and African American history and culture in specific disciplines and across the curriculum and to draw on contemporary issues and challenges encountered by African Americans.

Professional development programs should provide opportunities to draw on the knowledge and experience of African American scholars and community leaders as well as educators and administrators who have been successful in the school and classroom. Colloquia, workshops, and visiting lectureships offer the means to create these opportunities.

In addition, the curriculum should include research on culture and learning style and case studies of teachers who have been effective in a variety of cultural settings. Courses should prepare educators to use strategies and methods that have been validated as effective in raising the achievement of all students and particularly, low-performing students, including peer tutoring, cooperative learning, and accelerated learning.

Professional training should include study of the language spoken by the majority of African American students and should recognize that this language embodies a framework of communication styles, intonation, body language, structure, and grammar. Educators should be able to draw on this language as a resource in developing students' Standard English skills.

The professional development curriculum should provide opportunities to reflect on the powerful influences of expectations and attitudes, including ethnocentrism, on educators' behaviors. The guiding principle underlying professional development should be that the best education for all students is the type of instruction usually reserved for so-called gifted and talented students.

Although research has underscored the importance of parent involvement in education, professional development programs in colleges and universities have not responded by helping educators to cultivate skills and competencies necessary for effective communication and cooperation with African American families. Courses and practica must draw on real-life examples to illustrate strategies for planning and conducting parent-teacher meetings and open houses.

Educators should be prepared to draw on research and practical experience regarding factors that inhibit the school participation of many African American parents or families: for example, inflexible schedules for parent-teacher meetings, previous negative school experience, staff hostility, and fear of appearing stupid.

Schools are counted on more and more to respond to social, health, and other needs of the students they serve. Internships and practica should prepare educators to identify and use community institutions and resources available in African American communities, including service networks and delivery systems.

Community institutions provide many opportunities to create linkages between academic disciplines and real-life applications. Professional development programs should include courses or practica focusing on community service, internships, apprenticeships, and volunteerism. Educators also need to know how to organize field trips and visitations to community institutions and organizations.

Inservice Professional Development

Educators of African American students should be certified and competent in their subject area. Too often, the least qualified educators are assigned to schools that serve a predominantly African American population. Where educators are ill-prepared, schools and school districts need to provide well-planned and coordinated inservice programs linked to specific competencies and instructional goals for the school and district.

Resources for professional development must be committed to schools that exhibit the greatest need as evidenced by the level of student achievement. In addition, goals and objectives for professional development must be linked to measures for accountability, including decisions about salary, promotion, and tenure for educators at all levels.

Inservice programs must continually support the ability of educators, and particularly educators who are new to the profession, to reflect and draw on effective models, strategies, and approaches, as well as the knowledge and expertise of educators who have been successful in raising student achievement or maintaining high levels of student performance. Such individuals should be featured as workshop or conference presenters. Their strategies and approaches should be highlighted in school and district publications. Wherever possible, they should be used as mentors to new educators or as master teachers.

Increased and effective parent and family involvement must be an ongoing theme of professional development. Along with effective local and national models, programs should use parent and community volunteers as speakers and resource people. Inservice programs must help educators to plan and implement a variety of strategies for parent or family and community involvement, for instance,

- Bringing in family members to provide role models and personal illustrations and testimonies regarding contemporary or historical events, current issues, and community challenges

- Organizing student recognition programs to highlight student work; involving parents and other community members in setting up and conducting recognition programs

- Developing special events, such as programs in local libraries or museums and obtaining family membership cards or reduced admissions

- Conducting field trips to community institutions, businesses, and other sites, using parent or family volunteers

The experiences of effective educators of African American students help to provide a vision for a new approach to professional development based on knowledge and respect. However, changes in professional development will only be accomplished through the cooperation and collaboration of public education's stakeholders, including families, educators, labor organizations, community organizations, and institutions of higher education.

■ Conclusion

As educators in the United States struggle with questions of reform and standards, the difficult question of the role of culture in the educational process should be revisited. What is the real role of culture in teaching and learning? Prevailing methods and strategies for teaching and learning appear to limit or destroy the passion for learning in some groups while simultaneously inspiring and reinforcing the desire to know in others.

Successful educators of African American children today recognize the important role of student culture and experience in educational reform and school restructuring. Current reform and restructuring initiatives provide a fertile ground for implementing what we know about culture and learning style and for redefining the learner's role from a passive recipient of information to an active participant in generating and using knowledge.

Higher standards, increased expectations for learning, respect for the experiences and culture that learners bring to the classroom, curricula that accurately portray the contributions of non-European cultures to all disciplines—these are tools that will help us instill a renewed sense of purpose for the great structure of education, and these are the bases for reaching education's unexplored frontier.

■ References

Adler, M. J. (1984). *The Paideia program: An educational syllabus.* New York: Macmillan.

Asante, M. (1995). *African American history: A journey of liberation.* Maywood, NJ: Peoples Publishing Group.

Cartwright, M., & D'Orso, M. (1993). *For the children: Lessons from a visionary principal.* New York: Doubleday.

Cohen, D. (1993). Schools begin to glean lessons from children who "defy the odds." *Education Week, 12*(37), 1.

Comer, J. (1988, November). Educating poor minority children. *Scientific American,* pp. 42-48.

Commission on Students of African Descent. (1996). *Professional preparation to improve curriculum and instruction in New York City public schools* (unpublished report). New York: New York City Board of Education.

Derman-Sparks, L. (1995). How well are we nurturing racial and ethnic diversity? In D. Levine, R. Lowe, R. Peterson, & R. Tenorio (Eds.), *Rethinking schools, an agenda for change* (pp. 17-22). New York: New York Monthly Review Press.

Foster, H. L. (1986). *Ribbin', jivin', and playin' the dozens.* Cambridge, MA: Ballinger.

Gay, G., & Gilbert, S., II. (1985). Improving the success in school of poor black children. *Phi Delta Kappan, 67*(2), 133-137.

Guild, P. (1994, April). The culture/learning style connection. *Educational Leadership,* 31-36.

Hale, J. (1982). *Black children: Their roots, culture, and learning styles.* Provo, UT: Brigham Young University Press.

Harris, L., & Associates. (1992). *Metropolitan Life survey of the American teacher.* New York: Metropolitan Life Insurance Company.

Hilliard, A. (1995, November). *Teacher education from an African American perspective.* Paper presented to the conference on Defining the Knowledge Base for Urban Teacher Education, Emory University, Atlanta, GA.

Hollins, E., & Nobles, W. (1993). *Understanding African American culture and educating African American children: A teacher's guide.* San Francisco: California State University, San Francisco, Center for Applied Cultural Studies and Educational Achievement.

Jackson, S. A. (1990). *Accelerating academic achievement or poor black students: Transforming the teaching-learning environment and behaviors to accommodate the preferred learning styles of African American children.* Washington, DC: ERIC. (ERIC Reproduction Service No. 337 625)

Ladson-Billings, G. (1994). *The dreamkeepers.* San Francisco: Jossey-Bass.

Levin, H. M. (1990, April). *Accelerated schools: The inquiry process and the prospects for school change.* Paper presented at the annual meeting of the American Educational Research Association, Boston, MA.

Matthews, J. (1988). *Escalante: The best teacher in America.* New York: Holt, Rinehart.

National Alliance of Black School Educators. (1984, November). *Saving the African American child.* Washington, DC: Task Force on Black Academic and Cultural Excellence.

Nobles, W. (1994, May). Understanding African-American culture: A Teacher's guide. *CACSEA News, 2*(1), 2.

Nobles, W., & Mann, A. (1995). *Achieving academic and cultural excellence for African American students.* San Francisco: California State University, San Francisco, Center for Applied Cultural Studies and Educational Achievement.

Pasteur, A. B., & Toldson, I. L. (1982). *Roots of soul: The psychology of black expressiveness.* Garden City, NY: Anchor Press/Doubleday.

Ploumis-Devick, E., & Follman, J. (1993). *Appreciating differences: Teaching and learning in a culturally diverse classroom.* Greensboro, NC: South Eastern Regional Vision for Education.

Shabazz, A. (n.d). *African foundations of mathematics for curricula content.* Paper presented at the Second National Conference on the Infusion of African and African American Content in the School Curriculum, Atlanta, GA.

Slavin, R. (1994). *Preventing early school failure: Research, policy and practice.* Boston: Allyn & Bacon.

Thompson, R. F. (1990). African survivals in the black Atlantic world. In A. G. Hilliard, L. Payton-Stewart, & L. O. Williams (Eds.), *Infusion of African and African-American Content in the school curriculum* (pp. 63-72). Proceedings of the First National Conference, October 1989. Morristown, NJ: Aaron Press.

Woodson, C. (1933). *The miseducation of the Negro.* Washington, DC: Associated Publishers.

5

The African Advantage

Using African Culture to Enhance Culturally Responsive Comprehensive Teacher Education

■ *Mwangaza Michael-Bandele*

Comprehensive teacher education refers to an educational process designed to produce educators prepared to meet not only the academic but the social, health, and other real-life needs students bring into the classroom. This notion has gained increased attention over the past decade, given a growing regard for the value of educating the full and complete student. In addition, the rising impact of social issues, such as violence, homelessness, and issues of health that include HIV-AIDS in schools, has underscored the need for comprehensive education. It's objective is to prepare teachers to recognize and attend to a wide range of students' needs in addition to the academic realm. By design, it is organized to respond to a full range of learning variables, which includes culture.

Comprehensive teacher education is interchangeably referred to by a number of terms that include *collaborative, interprofessional, and integrated preparation*. This expanded preparation of teachers may include, for example, interprofessional training with other helping professionals or internships that provide experiential learning in social and health agencies that serve children. Such training provides student educators with the skill and perspective of the social worker, the health care professional, or other helping professionals as to how that respective profession attends to issues of its domain. Because its design is determined by variables affecting school success, it can function as a versatile template for preparation, well suited to respond to culturally and otherwise diverse populations. In fact, by design, comprehensive preparation is compelled to consider a very broad definition of culture represented by the cumulative characteristics of students. It recognizes the inherent limitations of teaching students whose social, physical, and cultural welfare is ignored. It demands a respect for the impact of well-being on academic achievement. The intent of comprehensive preparation is to better serve the whole student. The value of the design is its dedication to considering the whole child.

Indeed, indigenous Africans have a long history of educating the complete student through an integrated process that promotes the responsibility and welfare of the community through collaborative interaction. This dedication to social responsibility reflects a school of thought that may well serve the current interest in comprehensive teacher education. Although American educators frequently quote the West African proverb, "It takes a village to raise a child," little investigation is evident that explores the collective African mindset that produced this wisdom. The opportunity to coordinate a national comprehensive teacher education demonstration model over a 3-year period provided useful insight into the preparation process and how it might benefit from the infusion of indigenous African learning strategies. Many tenets of the comprehensive approach to education are integral to traditional African culture and identifiable within African educational practices. An exploration of the African cultural context, as well as a look at some of the practices that sustain its logic, may be useful to developing culturally and socially responsive teacher education strategies. The intent of this chapter is to highlight the value of indigenous African culture and educational practice in advancing comprehensive teacher preparation.

■ African Cultural Context

To speak of a singular African culture affirms a cultural homogeneity that is often negated in literature. Often and erroneously portrayed as a montage of unconnected people and cultures, there is a distinct and common cultural thread evident throughout much of indigenous African societies (Diop, 1978; Hilliard, 1995, p. 88). The commonality of cultures are often disguised beneath languages that sound different yet reflect common values, the practice of rituals that look different yet accomplish similar goals, and educational processes of varied forms that are ultimately designed to produce capable and socially responsible adults sufficiently skilled and motivated to contribute to the well-being of their respective societies (Moore, 1984; Neve, 1994; Ouzts, 1986; Rosenthal, 1991; Short, 1985; Tedla, 1995).

Social responsibility is an overriding objective in African education. It emphasizes the development of functional principles and values that subordinates the individual to the community. This process compels the individual to acquire skills that enable persons to readily recognize the value of others and to interact with others in such a way that enhances their unique good. This interactive approach affirms the value of individuals through the process of forging a harmonious community. Similarly, the comprehensive teacher preparation process intends to prepare teachers to approach teaching with an increased range of abilities that enables them to readily recognize the value of students, despite any immediate needs or challenges the student may have. The teacher is then prepared to interact with the student in such a way that minimizes barriers to learning while promoting the student's success. (Brandon & Meuter, 1995, p. 8; Bucci & Reitzammer, 1992, p. 292).

The African perspective of the preferred relationship between the individual and the group has logical origins. As the oldest racial-cultural group of all humankind, thousands of years of experience, intense observation, and the natural learning process of trial and error have taught the African that there is a distinct and preferred order for all things. Where human interaction is concerned, the sanctity of the individual is best preserved by the status and well-being of the community. The value of individual attainment in the African context is only the beginning of a self-development process. The process is completed, and therefore worthwhile, when the individual furthers the welfare of its community (Mulago, 1990, p. 121). The difference between the African and Western value of the individual is that the point of individual attainment within the Western context ends with the individual. This individualism creates tension with commitment to the community (Reed, 1995, p. 256). The African concept of cooperation and collaboration do not negate the value of the individual but rather, place the individual in context. The extent to which the individual is valuable has to do with the extent of her or his positive effect on others. The rights of the individual do not precede the rights and privilege of the community (Tedla, 1995, p. 30).

It is this philosophical framework that produced innumerable teaching and learning strategies that fostered an educational process focused on the enrichment of individual character that would promote selfless behavior. Indigenous educational processes reflected learning strategies that developed and transferred skills in harmonious human interaction aimed at strengthening and developing, first and foremost, the community. The community of Africans refers to a closely bonded collective. This fused collective "we" is captured in the edict, "I am because we are and since we are, therefore I am" (Mbiti, 1970, p. 141).

As an exemplary indigenous African educational system, Ancient Kemet (Egypt) may be the most significant of African societies to identify in a discussion on successful comprehensive education practices. Its process of teaching and learning laid the foundation for Egypt's unparalleled contributions to world civilization. The collaborative, integrated, comprehensive perspective common to African systems of education is rooted in Kemet. Hilliard (1995) states,

> Its philosophical origins are attributed to . . . the long, painstaking study of everything in nature that led Kemites and other Africans to the belief in the essential unity of all things in the universe. . . . This belief was held in KMT from earliest times. It was the ancient Kemites' attempt to live in harmony with nature's principles . . . that led them to develop the earliest moral teachings. . . . Kemetic education can be described as "functional," a blend of "theory and practice, a holistic education." (p. 124)

The ancient Kemites observed movement within nature, change, and life itself. What seems to have impressed them most was the degree to which a grand design appeared to be evident throughout the universe, enabling one who studied any part of the universe to understand the rest of it through analogies. For example, the Nile was a river on the earth, and the Milky Way was a "river in the sky." The observation of plant and animal life provided the opportunity to reflect on human life as well as with cycles of birth, growth, death, decay, and rebirth (Hilliard, 1995, p. 91). The observation of harmonious interaction in nature appears to have provided the logical rationale for modeling human interaction. Simply put, the cooperation evident in nature worked. It was consistent and effective in achieving interdependency that furthered existence.

This logic appears to have laid the formula for the rich philosophical underpinnings of comprehensive education. The object of interaction was, then, not a strategy for addressing problems or to serve as a learning conduit by which data could be transferred. The objective of indigenous African educational systems was cooperative, comprehensive interaction itself. The process represented and fostered the essential and core knowledge base needed to advance the group (Griaule, 1980).

■ African Learning Strategies

Use of Proverbs

Within the African context, the purpose of education is directed to the moral development of individuals committed to the well-being of the community. The acquisition of knowledge and skill is valuable to the extent that it enables the individual to harmoniously interact with others and in so doing, promote the group. Ultimately, knowing how to orchestrate human interaction and functional relationships that promote individual growth and development is at the foundation of successful learning. One effective means by which this collaborative educational philosophy is disseminated is through proverbs. Proverbs "not only show the mode of thought and the general principles used to direct personal and social behavior, but they also reveal the way Africans look upon the tangled web of human relationship and life" (Dzobo, 1975, p. viii). Africa's educational system is full of proverbs that direct the moral behavior of its people. Unlike the Western perspective of proverbs, which generally recognizes them as witty complements of prose, proverbs are integral components within African languages. Among the Ewe people of West Africa, many of whom reside in the modern-day nations of Ghana and Togo, proverbs are intricately woven into the language as essential components of communication. A person's maturity, intelligence, and ability to affect others favorably is often reflected in the skill and ease with which he or she commands the use of proverbs in conversation. This dual emphasis on understanding the meaning of proverb and exercising skill to use proverb appropriately to positively affect others represents the intent of the African educational process in microcosm: to learn both the tools and how to use them to benefit others.

As proverbs are integral to the language, their effect transcends all societal distinctions, such as age or gender or one's general station in life. If you speak the language, which is the carrier of the culture, you engage the messages contained in proverbs. The moral teachings of Ewe proverbs form an integral part of the Ewe language and are used not as rules or laws but as a means of self-expression. Like vocabulary, proverbs are a part of the collective mind of the people and are used as dictated by situational behavior. The principles and values represented in proverbs are intended to guide the conduct of those who know them and those who hear and understand them. Unlike rules or laws that are often memorized out of context, proverbs are introduced to highlight appropriate and inappropriate behavior, quite often when the behavior occurs. Hence, the use of proverbs functions as a powerful teaching tool to foster cooperative interaction (Dzobo, 1972, p. 86). Dzobo interprets the Ewe proverb, " One big tree does not make a forest," to mean that there is strength in unity and cooperative effort. The proverb stresses the importance of collective effort in achieving objectives and can be taken as a motto of community work. The proverb, "Voice in the village launches a boat," refers to "voice as the equivalent to the Latin expression *vox populi*, which stands for all the people living in the community and their joint effort." The proverb means that much could be achieved through joint effort. It is therefore used as a warning for people who are divided and not willing to work together. That "The thumb alone cannot press down the strings of the *Adondo* drum" (p. 40) is a reminder that what can be accomplished by many is impossible for one. *Adondo* or *dondo* is an elongated wooden drum with a narrow middle and can be played from both ends. The ends are joined by a series of strings, and the drummer plays the drum from under his arm and presses down the strings to vary its tone. Because the strings are many and are arranged in a circular form, it takes more than one thumb to press down all the strings. This proverb, and the ones like it, teach the importance of communal effort that is used to get things done in the village community (Dzobo, 1975).

"The anthill cannot ask the earth to push away in order to increase its size" is another way of saying that the individual is not greater than the group; even if he or she becomes very wealthy, his or her achievement comes through the fact that he or she is a member of a particular society. The proverb teaches people to have respect for the family and the social groups because they derive their being and living through them. It can also be said to be a way of admonishing people not to think too highly of themselves (Dzobo, 1975, p. 78). "If the nose is punched, the mouth is the cause" is a reminder that in any society, the wrong deeds of its individual members may affect all others, and so each must be his or her brother's or sister's keeper (p. 142).

"Cloth woven by two stupid [incompetent] weavers is enough for an expectant woman to wear" again expresses that there is strength in unity and cooperation. Although it underscores the need for unity and cooperation among people, it stresses that if two "stupid" persons have enough sense to work together to weave a substantial amount of cloth, one large enough even for a pregnant woman, then surely all others would have sense enough to work cooperatively in a similar manner (Dzobo, 1975, p. 178).

These proverbs do not only show the mode of thought and the general principles used to direct personal and social behavior, but they also reveal the way Africans look at human relationships and suggest ways for navigating the human environment. Most of the proverbs show the necessity for cultivating a capacity for deep sensitivity toward others that enables one to know the type of behavior that promotes harmony and the actions that hurt the feelings of others. This sensitivity engenders actions that express concern and respect for people. Proverbs are themselves composed by the reflective and observant moral teachers of the society and are collectively owned by the society and not by any particular individuals (Dzobo, 1975, p. xi).

Traditional society expects each member to become independent because it builds up one's self-respect and wins the respect of others. Therefore, the manner in which people are assisted must be in a way that is not derogatory or humiliating. The proverb, "The merciful may turn easily into enemies," warns that would-be helpers should be careful not to help others in such a way that in the end, their help is not wanted (Dzobo, 1972, p. 92). In other words, the giving person who has a less than mutually respectful attitude toward the person being assisted may well do more harm than good. That "the merciful may turn easily into enemies" is a reminder that to simply give to others is not enough. The person giving does not then have any right to treat the recipient with any less regard. The manner in which assistance is offered must be respectful and mutually dignified.

This proverb is particularly important within the context of Western formal education where professional and socioeconomic attainment is often confused with human worth. In the design of comprehensive teacher preparation programs, university and community relationships are typically directed by the university. Care should be taken to establish a reciprocal exchange that does not simply include community representation but balances the influence and power of community and university equally.

In addition, one of the rationales that most often drives the comprehensive teacher preparation effort is the need to address the social ills reflected by students in the classroom. These students are often referred to as the "disadvantaged," the "underclass," and most popular, "at-risk." Each of these terms, in varying degrees, characterizes the student as deficit. Each of these terms suggest the need to fix or compensate for some aspect of a child that is dysfunctional or missing. These terms can have the effect, consciously or subconsciously, of devaluing students and therefore, negatively affect a teacher's perspective of students who are given such labels. Teacher perception affects teacher expectation. An abundance of research affirms the overwhelming impact of teacher expectation on student performance (Moore, 1984; Ouzts, 1986; Rosenthal, 1991; Short, 1985). Hence, a rationale is needed for comprehensive teacher preparation that focuses less on students "at-risk" and more on teachers "at-work," assuming the professional responsibility to develop the knowledge base that allows them to recognize the multiple ways all children learn and develop the skill that permits teachers to build on the diverse learning modalities students inevitably bring to the classroom. This proverb, that "the merciful may turn easily into the enemies," is a poignant reminder that the most effective comprehensive, interprofessional teacher preparation process will train teachers to engage each student's needs not as barriers to teaching but rather as thoroughfares to effective learning. This perspective affirms the unconditional support of "the village" on behalf of the child.

Rites of Passage

Another integral component of the African educational system is the rites of passage. These rituals, although organized in different geographic locales by their respective communities, institutionalize the transmission of essential cultural knowledge to members of the community at appropriate developmental stages. Rites of passage are often organized around age groups. Members of the same age group, for instance, will experience rites of passage into adolescence, adulthood, or eldership together. In addition to conveying a core knowledge to the community, age group rites bind peers into a mutually obligating relationship much like biological siblings. Kenyatta (1965), in referencing age groups among the Gikuyu of East Africa, indicates that

The fellowship and unity of these age groups is a rather remarkable thing. . . . The age groups do more than bind men of equal standing together. . . . The whole organization of the community again enforces the lesson that behavior to other persons is what matters most. (Kenyatta, 1965, p. 112)

The process of learning to regard others respectfully and to conduct oneself in a manner that would promote harmony was grounded in hands-on practice:

Children learn this habit of communal work like others, not by verbal exhortations so much as by joining the older people in such social services. They see the household and friends building a house for somebody. . . . They go with their relatives to help in another man's garden. . . . All help given in this way is voluntary, and kinsfolk are proud to help one another. There is no [monetary] payment or expectation of payment. The whole thing rests on the principle of reciprocal obligation. . . . The selfish or self-regarding man has no name or reputation in Gikuyu community. An individualist is looked upon with suspicion. (p. 117)

In Gikuyu community, there is no really individual affair, for everything has a moral and social reference. In spite of the foreign elements that work against many of the Gikuyu institutions and the desire to implant the system of wholesale Westernization, this system of mutual help and the tribal solidarity in social services, political, and economic activities is still maintained by a large proportion of the Gikuyu people. It is less practiced among those Gikuyu who have been Europeanized or tribalized (Kenyatta, 1965).

The striking thing in the Gikuyu system of education, and the feature that most sharply distinguishes it from the European system of education, is the primary place given to personal relations.

Europeans assume that, given the right knowledge and ideas, personal relations can be left largely to take care of themselves, and this is perhaps the most fundamental difference in outlook between Africans and Europeans. We may sum it up by saying that to the Europeans, "Individuality is the ideal of life," to the African the ideal is the right relations with, and behavior to other people. (Kenyatta, 1965, p. 118)

Implementing African Stratagems

The opportunity to coordinate four comprehensive teacher education demonstration programs over a 3-year period provided useful insight into the comprehensive preparation process and how it might benefit from the infusion of African learning strategies. Although geographically diverse and representative of a wide range of programmatic approaches, the sites shared common victories as a result of meeting common challenges. Each success was dependent on the extent to which program participants skillfully minimized individual objectives on behalf of the collective agenda. These agendas entailed levels of cooperation not normally required of faculty members at the university. Shared budgets, office space, and interprofessional course offerings that included students and faculty from as many as five different schools representing five different academic disciplines are a few of the ways in which program participants collaborated to prepare teachers and other helping professionals in an expanded interprofessional way. The usefulness of a comprehensive integrative conceptual framework that not only (a) cultivates the notion of comprehensiveness but also (b) expands the common paradigm and (c) offers methods for teaching and learning may be very helpful to the development of this strategy in U.S. education. The African context offers useful examples that further the understanding of the value of comprehensive teacher education and provides an example of teaching methods that may be transferable to the formal educational environment.

There are immediate similarities and obvious differences between comprehensive teacher preparation in higher education and the indigenous African comprehensive learning process. Although teacher preparation is designed to equip teachers with skills to effectively attend to the wide range of health, social, and other needs of students in school, the comprehensive African learning process prepares individuals to fulfill a social and ethical obligation to advance all members of the community. The expanded African perspective provides insight into what may occur within teacher education at a more entrenched African-influenced "next level" of conceptualization and implementation. This "African level" encourages a personal obligation to comprehensive teacher preparation that would drive professional commitment. The examples that follow overlay African thought and practice atop current education practice used in comprehensive-collaborative teacher education preparation.

Student Education Cohorts

Prospective education, health, and social science practitioners are grouped together so that they share an interprofessional classroom and practicum experiences. As a cohort, these students are identified as a cohesive working entity expected to maintain a close and interactive relationship that transcends the typical relationship of classmates. Their close physical and conceptual proximity is intended to stimulate caring relationships that magnify professional interaction and delivery (Noddings, 1995, p. 366). The intent is to foster a greater and therefore deeper level of interaction that would facilitate shared professional perspectives that address the best ways of attending to multiple needs of classroom students. This teacher education strategy is akin to the process of establishing African age groups. As detailed earlier, age groups are vital and very powerful units within society that nourish relationships that are no less committed than the bond between biological siblings. Aspects of the African process of solidifying the age grade that may be useful in fostering student education cohorts include

- Expanded lengths of time (at least two, rather than one semester) in which the cohorts are assembled. The amount of time spent interacting has an obvious direct bearing on the level of group interprofessional exchange.
- Ongoing opportunities where the cohort is publicly identified as one cohesive body. Creating expectation beyond a course grade (within the university and wider community) is intended to translate into greater buy-in on the part of students than is typically associated with formal learning.
- Coordination of the comprehensive-interprofessional professorate and administrators as a distinct entity, identifiable as the "senior age group," which models the interaction expected of the interprofessional student cohort.

The logical and practical extension of the student cohort is the inservice teacher cohort where rather than learning separately, inservice teachers learn together. This inservice extension of comprehensive preparation would address the pervasive problem of classroom teacher isolation, lending itself to the development of a more communal exchange between teachers (Dilworth & Imig, 1995, p. 7).

Community Institutionalization

Discussions about institutionalizing comprehensive teacher preparation are typically concerned with ways in which this approach can become infused within the academy. A paradigm shift that views institutionalization as a process best entrenched in the community would represent the African cultural perspective that defines the principal responsibility of all educational sources as working on behalf of the community. Hence, the logical physical and ideological location of an effort designed to prepare teachers is where the classroom students are found. This location would not, by design, negate any simultaneous activity at the university but would create an opportunity to extend and enhance its effectiveness. Those opportunities may include

- Teacher education training centers permanently located at social service agencies, health facilities, community schools (professional development schools), recreation centers, or churches. Any or all of these community institutions where children are served are well entrenched in the natural learning environment, representing a rich source of practical learning and application.

- Increased opportunity to engage the significant persons in the life of a child, thereby increased opportunity to make valuable linkages toward understanding and therefore, genuinely respecting the child

- A teacher education process less dependent on the singular and oftentimes culturally estranged academic perspective, which invites programmatic direction from the cumulative wisdom of the community. This design may diminish the perspective of student, family, and community as "clients" and create a check and balance between the university and the community independent of the whims of altruism.

- An environment where teacher education students can observe classroom students in their "natural environment" and subsequently develop practical culture-specific and environment-specific approaches that correspond to the needs of students.

Darling-Hammond, Dilworth, and Bullmaster (1997) underscore the importance of incorporating a function of community into the teaching-learning process in describing successful culturally responsive teaching strategies where "teachers built relationships in their classrooms that were marked by social equality, egalitarianism, and mutuality stemming from a group, rather than an individual ethos" (p. 6).

Consensus Building

If the cornerstone of comprehensive teacher education rests on the extent to which student educators are trained in a manner that models and promotes harmonious and collaborative teaching and learning, then its success is determined by the level of cooperative synergy generated by its teacher education facilitators and other partnering participants. There is a body of skills essential to advancing collaboration. Among them, the ability to communicate in such a way that fosters a genuine desire among people to work together is perhaps the most important. That skill may be enhanced by the African approach to group decision making. For instance, the ability to determine group decision by process of democratic consensus that considers the opinion of all group members is preferred within the African context to group decisions determined by the numeric majority, whereby the majority rules. Although the majority-rule process does not give significant consideration to the disposition of the numerical minority who are left to be "ruled," it is considered democratic and fair by Western standards. Within the indigenous African context where the value of the group supersedes the value of the individual or any smaller unit, group decision making must take into account the appeasement of any segment of the group that is not in agreement with the larger entity. Thus, considerable time is spent negotiating group decisions. Although the outcome may be evident fairly early in the negotiation process, the discussion may continue for an extended period of time when the numeric minority has the opportunity to fully express its position of dissent. Fellow group members are compelled not only to listen with genuine interest but to extend words of regret that the dissenters' opinion will not prevail. These gestures are intended to minimize any differences among the group and to take care that each group member, of both the numeric majority and minority, leave the decision-making process with his or her sense of dignity and respect intact. Hence, considerable time is spent not simply at arriving at a group decision but engaging in an extended process that preserves and advances group integrity.

Comprehensive teacher preparation programs could benefit from a more expanded "African capacity" for consensus building that may foster greater collaborative and interprofessional collegiality.

■ Conclusion

Identifying African resources well suited to inform the U.S. system of education is part of a larger growing body of knowledge that recognizes the value of other cultures, often indigenous to people of color, that have been diminished largely as a result of European hegemony. The 1991 *Times* magazine cover story "Lost Tribes, Lost Knowledge" discusses the value of knowledge and the general wealth of "wisdom and expertise" contained in traditional cultures that the Western world sometimes denigrates and often ignores. *Times* author Eugene Linden (1991) states,

> Over the ages, indigenous peoples have developed innumerable technologies and arts. Much of this expertise and wisdom has already disappeared, and if neglected, most of the remainder could be gone within the next generation. Until recently, few in the developed world cared much about this cultural holocaust. If this knowledge had to be duplicated from scratch, it would beggar the scientific resources of the West. . . . Some scientists are beginning to recognize that the world is losing an enormous amount of basic research as indigenous people lose their culture and traditions. Scientists may someday be struggling to reconstruct this body of wisdom to secure the developed world's future. (p. 48)

Although Linden's remarks are largely concerned with the field of science, the same argument has merit outside of science. Given that many of these cultures are chronologically older than European culture, it would stand to reason that where people have had the longest amount of time and sufficient opportunity to exercise the process by which knowledge is often identified—trial and error—that people will develop knowledge that others who have existed for fewer years have not. That research identifies African people as the first of all humankind should help to explain why Africans have developed systems of education and socialization that Westerners, including U.S. Americans, may learn from. African and other group-centered cultures may hold a plethora of concepts and educational practices valuable to the national effort to educate the whole child and the specific concern of this paper, comprehensive teacher preparation. Hallinger, Chantarapanya, Taraseina, and Srliboonma (1996) remind us that

> Much of the world looks toward North America for models of sound educational practice. . . . There is much that Western educators can

learn from other countries. Too often, the exchange of information is one-way: from North American (and Europe) to other countries." (p. 25)

Exploration of educational practices among other cultures may be particularly appropriate as the search for more culturally responsive teaching and learning strategies accelerates. Westerners, then, including Americans, may be wise to follow the lead of one of their most revered ancestral groups, the Greeks, to whom the founding of Western civilization is often attributed, who frequently studied the successful practices of Africans to learn that which they had yet to know (Bernal, 1990; Diop, 1974; Hilliard, 1995; James, 1954).

■ References

Bernal, M. (1990). *Black Athena: The Afroasiatic roots of classical civilization.* New Brunswick, NJ: Rutgers University Press.

Brandon, R., & Meuter, L. (1995). *Proceedings: National conference on interprofessional education and training.* Seattle: University of Washington, Human Services Policy Center.

Bucci, J., & Reitzammer, A. F. (1992). Collaboration with health and social service professionals: Preparing teachers for new roles. *Journal of Teacher Education, 43,* 290-296.

Darling-Hammond, L., Dilworth, M., & Bullmaster, M. (1997). *Educators of color: The recruitmant, preparation, and retention of persons of color in the teaching profession.* Washington, DC: U.S. Department of Education, Office of Educational Research and Improvement.

Dilworth, M., & Imig, D. (1995). Professional teacher development. *The ERIC Review, 3*(3), 7.

Diop, C. A. (1974). *The African origin of civilization: Myth or reality.* Westport, CT: Lawrence Hill.

Diop, C. A. (1978). *The cultural unity of black Africa.* Chicago: Third World Press.

Dzobo, N. K. (1972). *Moral value of Ewe proverbs.* Accra, Ghana: Waterville.

Dzobo, N. K. (1975). *African proverbs: Guide to conduct, Vol. 2.* Accra, Ghana: Waterville.

Griaule, M. (1980). *Conversations with Ogotemmeli.* Oxford: Oxford University Press.

Hallinger, P., Chantarapanya, P., Taraseina, P., & Srliboonma, U. (1996). Nourishing the spirit: The role of ritual in building communities of learners. *Journal of Staff Development, 17,* 22-25.

Hilliard, A. G. (1995). *The maroon within us.* Baltimore: Black Classic Press.

James, G. G. M. (1954). *Stolen legacy.* Nashville, TN: James C. Winston.

Kenyatta, J. (1965). *Facing Mt. Kenya.* New York: Vintage.

Linden, E. (1991, September 23). Lost tribes, lost knowledge. *Time,* pp. 46-61.

Mbiti, J. (1970). *African religions and philosophy.* New York: Doubleday.

Moore, D. W. (1984) Disparate teacher attention favoring the more able: Some data from Papau New Guinean community and provincial high schools. *Australian Journal of Education, 28*(2), 154-164.

Mulago, V. (1990). Africa and Christianity. In J. Olupona (Ed.), *African traditional religions in contemporary society.* New York: Paragon House.

Neve, H. T. (Ed.). (1994). *Homeward journey: Readings in African studies.* Trenton, NJ: Africa World Press.

Noddings, N. (1995). A morally defensible mission for schools in the 21st century. *Phi Delta Kappan, 76*(5), 365-368.

Ouzts, D. T. (1986). Teacher expectation: Implications for achievement. *Reading Horizons, 26*(2), 133-139.

Reed, G. G. (1995). Looking in the Chinese mirror: Reflecting on moral-political education in the United States. *Educational Policy, 9*(3), p. 256.

Rosenthal, R. (1991). Teacher expectancy effects: A brief update 25 years after the Pygmalion experiment. *Journal of Research in Education, 1*(1), 3-12.

Short, G. (1985). Teacher expectation and West Indian underachievement. *Educational Research, 27*(2), 95-110.

Tedla, E. (1995). *Sankofa: African thought and education.* New York: Peter Lang.

Multicultural Content Infusion by Student Teachers

Perceptions and Beliefs of Cooperating Teachers

- *Michael Vavrus*
- *Mustafa Ozcan*

Nationally, educators continually stress the need for preservice teachers to gain familiarity and competence for infusing multicultural content into the curriculum for kindergarten through 12th grade. Embedded within this expectation is the desire to have a teaching force with a deeper understanding of the relationship of the school curriculum to a pluralistic society (Tyson, 1994; Zimpher & Ashburn, 1992). For teachers to interact effectively with diverse cultural groups outside the standard school boundaries, they must hold a knowledge base sensitive to the conditions of people historically placed on the margins of society's political and economic activities (Collins, 1993).

How to reach the goal of a culturally responsive teaching force through teacher education remains enigmatic. For prospective teachers gaining appropriate pedagogical skills in multicultural education, an introductory experience through one course in the teacher preparation curriculum appears inadequate (Bennett, 1989; Bliss, 1990; McDiarmid

& Price, 1990). Even when multicultural information that reduces the stereotyping attitudes of preservice teachers is included in the teacher preparation curriculum (Tran, Young, & DiLella, 1994), both student teachers and practitioners generally do not demonstrate competence in applying a curricular knowledge base with multiple perspectives and the interconnectedness of various cultures' histories (Banks, 1993b, 1994; Garcia & Pugh, 1992; Vavrus, 1994). Research is inconclusive on the added value of multicultural education when teaching experiences with culturally diverse student populations are taken into account (Brown & Kysilka, 1994; Grant & Secada, 1990; Rios, 1991).[1] Compounding this dilemma is the continuing dominance of an Eurocentric orientation toward schooling that either excludes or places on the curricular margins multicultural content (Banks, 1993b, 1994; Collins, 1993; Estrada & McLaren, 1993; Gollnick, 1992b; Irvine, 1992; Martin, 1991; McCarthy, 1994; Watkins, 1994).

Few studies and reviews are available that analyze the multicultural education pedagogy of teacher preparation programs when delivered throughout an entire curriculum and into the student teaching phase (Gollnick, 1992a; Grant & Secada, 1990; Mason, 1987; Ramsey, Vold, & Williams, 1989; Spears, Oliver, & Maes, 1990). Although research data are also limited on how cooperating teachers interpret the infusion of multicultural content into the school curriculum by student teachers, Haberman and Post (1990) indicate that multicultural orientations of cooperating teachers are skewed to individualistic, psychological models rather than toward group or societal perspectives. During student teaching, cooperating teacher attitudes toward multicultural education affect the context in which student teachers must enact lessons with multicultural content (Garcia & Pugh, 1992; Nel, 1992). A more thorough understanding of how cooperating teachers approach multicultural education would provide teacher education programs an increased understanding of the classroom setting where multicultural content infusion is an expectation for student teachers (Goodwin, 1994; Grant & Secada, 1990) and would serve as an information source for programs seeking field sites conductive to the development of multicultural competencies for preservice teachers (Haberman & Post, 1990).

■ Purpose and Theoretical Framework

Learning how cooperating teachers think about multicultural content infusion by student teachers is the purpose of the study discussed in this

chapter. Our study has two primary dimensions: (a) determining cooperating teachers' perceptions of the orientations for infusing multicultural content into the curriculum by student teachers and (b) ascertaining
cooperating teachers' beliefs on the appropriate level for student teachers to infuse multicultural content. Often, multicultural approaches are
undifferentiated, enabling practitioners to report a high correlation between their preservice experiences in multicultural education and their
eventual instructional strategies in teaching assignments without regard
to the nature of the multicultural content (see McDaniel, McDaniel, &
McDaniel, 1988). To distinguish more clearly the multicultural curriculum orientations of cooperating teachers, we chose "Levels of Integration of Multicultural Content" by James Banks (1988; 1993a, Chapter 10)
as the theoretical framework for analyzing the cooperating teachers' beliefs and perceptions. This theoretical construct involves four levels of
approach:

1. Contributions: focuses on heroes, holidays, and individual cultural events
2. Additive: adds content, concepts, themes, and perspectives to the
   curriculum without changing its structure
3. Transformational: changes the structure of the curriculum to enable students to view concepts, issues, events, and themes from
   the perspective of females and diverse ethnic and cultural
   groups
4. Social action: enables students to make decisions on important
   social issues and take actions to solve them (Banks, 1988, 1993a)

In a hierarchical order of complexity and quality, beginning with the
contributions approach and moving up to social action, these four
abstract categories were used as ideal types (Weber, 1978). Though these
levels are presented in their pure forms, they may overlap or be blended
by teachers in actual teaching situations (Banks, 1993a).

When teachers adopt a contributions approach, the structure and
goals of the standard curriculum remain unchanged. This level is frequently used when a teacher first attempts to integrate multicultural
content into the curriculum because it is the easiest for teachers to use.
The next level, the additive approach, as its name implies, adds multicultural content to the curriculum while maintaining a mainstream perspective (Banks, 1993a). The transformative approach, however, represents a move toward academic knowledge that

consists of concepts, paradigms, themes, and explanations that challenge mainstream academic knowledge and that expand the historical literary canon . . . [under the assumption] that knowledge is not
neutral but is influenced by human interests, that all knowledge reflects the power and social relationships within society, and that an
important purpose of knowledge construction is to help people improve society. (Banks, 1993b, p. 9)

The highest level in Banks's model, social action, requires the
implementation of the theory of social reconstructionism (Zeichner,
1993) in the context of multicultural education (Grant & Secada, 1990).

■ Method

A survey instrument developed for qualitative analysis was sent to all
cooperating teachers in a teacher preparation program for the 1993-1994
academic year. Of 115 cooperating teachers, 95 surveys were completed
and returned (82.6%). The cooperating teachers provided supervision in
their classrooms for teacher education students from an institution in the
Midwest accredited as a consortium by the National Council for the Accreditation of Teacher Education. For more than 15 years, prospective
teachers have been required by the state to take a course devoted to multicultural and nonsexist education with a focus on creating positive attitudes among teacher candidates toward culturally diverse groups. Located in the region's primary urban center, the institution's service area
also includes accessible rural areas. The demographic composition of the
community reflects a 19th-century German and Irish Catholic heritage
that in recent years has experienced a growth in populations representing people of color.

The data we collected were qualitative in nature. Teachers answered
open-ended questions to reflect their perceptions and beliefs on the approaches for integrating multicultural content. They stated both their
ideas about approaches to multicultural education and their observations of student teachers in the infusion of multicultural content into the
standard curriculum. The data—that is, teachers' answers—were analyzed to discover the patterns in the infusion of multicultural content
into curriculum.

Provided with the four approaches and corresponding definitions,
cooperating teachers were first asked to identify "the approach(es) you
professionally judge that your student teacher used when infusing mul-

ticultural concepts into his or her lessons" and then to describe any difficulties they perceived their student teachers may have had with multicultural content infusion. The other part of the survey asked, "Which of the approaches do you, as a cooperating teacher, believe are most appropriate for student teachers to use?" with a follow-up opportunity to explain their respective reasoning for their responses.

Data were initially analyzed by scoring the number of responses in each of the four levels of multicultural content integration. First, cooperating teachers' perceptions of the actual level of infusion by student teachers were recorded followed by a noting of cooperating teachers' beliefs about the most appropriate level for student teachers to be using. Aggregated information was also analyzed according to the teaching assignments of cooperating teachers (i.e., regular or special education and grade level).

For the narrative data, content analysis was used to describe the relative frequency and importance of topics raised by the cooperating teachers. Tables were created to categorize these responses. The data in the tables represent the explanatory statements by cooperating teachers regarding any difficulties student teachers may have encountered in multicultural content infusion and the thinking of cooperating teachers on the most appropriate levels of multicultural curriculum integration for student teachers. Data were further analyzed by the level or approach cited by the cooperating teachers as well as their respective teaching areas and grade levels.

Cooperating teacher responses were also compared to an earlier study of actions and attitudes reported by student teachers in a similar survey (Vavrus, 1994). In that investigation, an analysis was conducted on a self-evaluation questionnaire related to a multicultural education performance indicator completed by student teachers in the same teacher education program from which the current sample of cooperating teachers was drawn. Data existed from the content analysis of the student teachers' self-evaluations suggesting that cooperating teacher pedagogical approaches may influence student teacher multicultural curriculum decisions, meriting a further comparison to the results of our current study.

■ Results

From the sample surveyed, 74% of the cooperating teachers indicated that student teachers use more than one approach. As seen in Table 6.1,

TABLE 6.1   Approaches Used by Student Teachers to Integrate
Multicultural Content Into Curriculum as Reported
by Cooperating Teachers

Assignment Level	Contributions Approach	Additive Approach	Transformation Approach	Social Action Approach	Total
PK-K, Regular Ed.	6	8	4	2	20
PK-K, Special Ed.	5	4	1	1	11
1-6, Regular Ed.	28	34	18	9	89
1-6, Special Ed.	5	5	5	5	20
7-12, Regular Ed.	19	22	9	7	57
7-12, Special Ed.	1	4	2	2	9
Total	64	77	39	26	206

NOTE: Total $N = 95$; total notations = 206.

the additive approach is noted most often and is followed closely by the contributions approach. The transformational and social action approach—third and fourth, respectively—were reported much less frequently. Nineteen percent of the sample noted that "all" or "any" of the approaches are appropriate for student teachers. Although not completely congruent, these results suggest a pattern similar to cooperating teacher beliefs on the ideal level for application by student teacher.

Of the cooperating teachers, 42% reported that student teachers have difficulty with multicultural content infusion. About an equal number of the total sample (17%) reported the source of the difficulty as either student teacher preparation in multicultural education or a combination of teacher perceptions centered around a limited time for meeting infusion expectations and negative attitudes toward multicultural education (see Table 6.2).

Mentioned the most frequently, the additive approach was considered the most appropriate level for student teachers by 45% of the cooperating teachers. At the other end of the spectrum, 18% of the teachers

TABLE 6.2 Source of Difficulties Student Teachers Encounter in Infusing Multicultural Content Into Curriculum as Reported by Cooperating Teachers

Assignment Level	Pupils' Mental and Social Characteristics	Limitations of Curriculum, Topic, or Time or a Combination of These	Lack of Knowledge and Experience of the Student Teacher	Negative Cooperating Teacher Beliefs About Multicultural Education	Total
PK-K, Regular Ed	—	2	2	—	4
PK-K, Special Ed.	2	—	—	1	3
1-6, Regular Ed.	—	—	9	2	11
1-6, Special Ed.	4	3	1	—	8
7-12, Regular Ed.	1	5	4	4	14
7-12, Special Ed.	—	—	—	—	—
Total	7	10	16	7	40

NOTE: Forty teachers out of 95 said that their student teachers had difficulties in infusing multicultural content into curriculum.

thought the transformative approach was suitable for student teaching. As indicated in Table 6.3, 19% of the cooperating teachers responded that "any" or "all" of the approaches are fitting for student teachers. These latter responses appear to stem from cooperating teachers confusing Banks's (1993a) curriculum approaches with either learning styles, such as a teacher reasoning that pupils "need various ways to learn," or teaching styles as evidenced by another teacher explaining that multicultural approaches ought to be determined by "whatever student teachers feel the most comfortable with and feel they are able to teach successfully."

Table 6.4 provides a breakdown of the four approaches according to the reasons teachers gave for favoring a particular level of multicultural content inclusion. The most common explanation, reported by cooperating teachers for favoring the additive and contributions levels, was based on ease of application into their previously designed curriculum plans. The second most frequent reason pertained to the belief in the appropriateness of multicultural content for the pupils of cooperating teachers. The least common rationale was their concern with the limited time for student teaching and the perceived competence of student teachers.

The reasons given by the cooperating teachers for selecting the transformational and social action levels tended to note neither ease of application nor the student teachers' competence. The one common refrain was that these levels were best for their pupils. The social action approach was perceived by the largest subset of cooperating teachers favoring this level as one that student teachers could accomplish. Most responses were unique and vague. That is to say, the rationale generally given by the cooperating teachers for their selecting the transformational and social action approaches were not similar to nor consistent with the reasons given by Banks (1993a) for selecting these levels.

▪ Discussion and Implications

A close examination of the qualitative research findings imply some potential shortcomings relevant to the multicultural education knowledge base held by cooperating teachers and conveyed to student teachers. Cooperating teachers appear more comfortable with the additive and contributions approaches that may mirror their overall backgrounds in multicultural education. Cooperating teachers also tend to lack consistent criteria in choosing the approaches for integrating multicultural content

TABLE 6.3 Most Appropriate Approach(es) for Student Teachers to Integrate Multicultural Content Into Curriculum as Reported by Cooperating Teachers

Assignment Level	Contributions	Additive	Transformational	Social action	All or Any	Others	Total
PK-K, Regular Ed	1	4	—	2	—	—	7
PK-K, Special Ed	3	3	—	—	—	—	6
1-6, Regular Ed	12	18	10	11	7	3	61
1-6, Special Ed	3	2	2	3	4	—	14
7-12, Regular Ed	7	14	5	7	7	2	42
7-12, Special Ed	—	11	—	2	1	—	14
Total	26	52	17	25	19	5	144

NOTE: Total N = 95, with 5 not responding to this item; total notations = 144.

TABLE 6.4 Cooperating Teachers' Reasons for Favoring Individual Approaches

Approach	Time Set for Student Teaching	Level of Student Teacher Competence	Beneficial for Pupils	Fits Curriculum	Ease of Application	Other	None	Total
Contributions	3	2	6	5	10	—	—	26
Additive	7	7	8	15	7	—	—	44
Transformational	—	—	4	3	—	4	6	17
Social action	—	—	8	2	1	—	5	16
Total	10	9	26	25	18	4	11	103

NOTE: From total $N = 95$, 90 teachers responded to this item; multiple approaches reported by cooperating teachers (see Table 6.1).

into the curriculum. The overall rationale for selecting the levels of multicultural content integration had less to do with curricular effectiveness and appropriateness for their pupils and more with issues of classroom efficiency, such as ease of application by the student teacher. The natures of the contributions and the additive approaches lend themselves to the least amount of curricular modification and may also account for the cooperating teachers' choice of these two approaches. For example, the additive approach was supported for one teacher because it "does not cause large disruptions to existing curriculum." This aspect of the study suggests that, in comparison to Banks's (1993a) hierarchy, cooperating teachers generally hold low expectations for student teachers' infusing multicultural content into the curriculum.

Cooperating teacher attitudes in these instances could be a function of the fact that an inadequate subject knowledge base, such as in multicultural education, results in inflexible curriculum implementation by teachers (Walker, 1990),[2] thus holding "a basic skills orientation to teaching that seems to render multicultural concerns superfluous" (Grant & Secada, 1990, p. 418). Limitations on the possibilities for multicultural content integration are further confounded by those cooperating teachers who view multicultural education as "not applicable" and feel "too pressed for time to just 'change' the curriculum to include MCNS [multicultural nonsexist] education." One declared, "Our students are starting to feel 'stuffed' with Multicultural Education; we can't do any more without facing a backlash!" Another recommended, "College professors ought to spend a few weeks in our junior highs and high schools to get a feel for what real problems we as teachers face, and I think you'll find Multiculturalism way down the list."

Cooperating teachers' reasoning for selecting the transformational and social action levels overall suggests that they do not understand the conceptual construct involved in transforming the curriculum (Banks, 1993b) and fail to grasp what social action actually means for the classroom curriculum. Cooperating teachers appear to lack a multicultural education grounding in the implications for critically transforming the curriculum to eventually include social action. Although cooperating teachers cite the appropriateness of the social action approach, the study shows no indication that social action activities as defined by Banks (1993a) and others (Grant & Secada, 1990; Zeichner, 1993) were actually being planned and enacted by student teachers. Because multicultural education is a continuing manifestation of the civil rights movement, change and action are embedded expectations of multicultural education and inherent contributors to tension with the conventional, Eurocentric academic curricula (Watkins, 1994). Because most teachers are less interested in curriculum development and "simply want a good set of written curriculum guidelines to use so that they can devote their attention to working with students" (Walker, 1990, pp. 229-230), cooperating teachers may perceive transformative approaches that require a fundamental change in the curriculum beyond the norm of their job role. "When the student teacher gets a full time job," reasoned a cooperating teacher, "he or she may not be able to make major changes in his or her curriculum." Consequently, cooperating teachers may not look at multicultural curriculum transformation and social activism as the job of the teacher and, therefore, see it as an inappropriate experience for individuals becoming teachers.

Because all student teachers take a course in multicultural education prior to student teaching, it is likely they were aware of the Banks's hierarchy for moving to the transformational and social action levels. However, the responses of the cooperating teachers coupled with other studies of student teacher multicultural content infusion (Garcia & Pugh, 1992; Vavrus, 1994) suggest that, regardless of student teachers' previous knowledge, student teachers tend to pick up the approach considered most important and practical by their cooperating teachers and are discouraged from attempting the higher levels of Banks's model. These factors may be attributed to cooperating teachers who impose their ideas of multicultural education on student teachers or to student teachers who look up to cooperating teachers as significant models of teaching or both. Either way, the beliefs of cooperating teachers about multicultural education appear as an influential variable on the teaching expectations and behaviors of student teachers.

The results of our study suggest that teacher education programs need to make operational to cooperating teachers expectations for multicultural content infusion during student teaching. For the preparation program used for this study, having 17% of the cooperating teachers consider student teacher preparation in the application of multicultural content as inadequate when aggregated across all approaches intimates that more attention is also needed in curriculum and instruction methodology courses to multicultural content integration in the design of lessons. One teacher, mindful of potential demands when moving up Banks's (1993a) hierarchy, pointed out that "transformational and social action require a great deal of planning that is not introduced in an effective manner in [the student teachers'] education (methods) courses." Realizing that the four approaches imply a sequence of developmental stages through which teachers may pass as they develop lessons with multicultural content, a cooperating teacher advised, "Student teachers need to work from the basics [e.g., additive level] so they can develop confidence through success. Too much experimentation [e.g., transformation] can lead to confusion and chaos." When working together on developing multicultural education competencies of preservice teachers, both teacher educators and cooperating teachers must initially take a collective shift in focus away from what is most efficient within a given classroom to what is most desirable and effective for pupils in a culturally diverse society.

A grasp of content infusion at the additive and contributions levels will demand less explanation than at the transformational and social action levels. Mindful of the history of the originators of social reconstructionism in the 1930s, teacher educators hoping for cooperating teachers to adopt a social-action approach on their own may again be a "miscalculation" founded on "an optimistic yet unfounded" (Watkins, 1991, p. 34) sense of teacher agency. Indeed, infusion at the latter two levels requires teacher educators to collaborate with cooperating teachers in a deeper exploration of what it means to approach curriculum transformation and social action from a critical orientation. A cooperating teacher sympathetic to the multicultural goal of social action cautioned that "this would take some years building."

Collaboration on multicultural education with cooperating teachers implies a long-term commitment mindful of the various constraints teachers work under when attempting to change their classroom curriculum (Walker, 1990, chap. 10). Collaboration also involves an understanding of cultural fits in a curriculum (Peshkin, 1992) as well as giving attention to the relationship that must evolve between teacher educators and cooperating teachers for teachers to realize the role of curriculum developer (Clandinin & Connelly, 1992). Collaboration between cooperating teachers and teacher educators on multicultural education is fraught with anxiety for providing an environment conducive for student teachers to become culturally responsive educators with their own pupils because, as Sleeter (1991) explains, "helping students articulate, critically examine, and develop their own beliefs and action agendas for emancipation of oppressed people is very difficult; it is not discussed sufficiently by multicultural education practitioners or theorists" (p. 22). Nevertheless, lasting benefits may begin to accrue to both teacher education programs and local school districts when beginning the process of collaboratively seeking to conceptualize multicultural content infusion around the model of Banks (1988, 1993a) for the purpose of widening the dialog on the meanings and interpretations of a multicultural curriculum for application by a new generation of teachers.

■ Notes

1. In a study of urban teachers in culturally diverse settings, Rios (1991) found that teachers were minimally engaged in multicultural education, leading him to conclude that "simply putting teachers in multicultural contexts is not going to guarantee a more sophisticated thinking about multicultural education" (pp. 194-195). Although Grant and Secada (1990) report that "experiences with representatives from diverse populations are worthwhile for teachers," they also caution that any positive gain seems "predicated on the student [teachers] and teachers having support mechanisms . . . [and] some external motivation for their efforts" (p. 418). This condition is reinforced by observations from Brown and Kysilka (1994) of a student teacher who failed to make apparently obvious connections with her unit on Mexico and the Mexican heritage of some of her students: "This student teacher most likely saw multicultural and global applications as a technical demand of the curriculum, not as an extension of pupils' learning or a celebration of an individual's background and culture" (p. 314).

2. Walker (1990) explains that "teachers whose knowledge of a topic is too limited can only implement a curriculum in a rigid way" (p. 359).

■ References

Banks, J. A. (1988). Approaches to multicultural curriculum reform. *Multicultural Leader, 1*(2), 1-4.

Banks, J. A. (1993a). Approaches to multicultural curriculum reform. In J. A. Banks & C. A. M. Banks (Eds.), *Multicultural education: Issues and perspectives* (pp. 195-214). Boston: Allyn & Bacon.

Banks, J. A. (1993b). The canon debate, knowledge construction, and multicultural education. *Educational Researcher, 22*(5), 4-14.

Banks, J. A. (1994). *An introduction to multicultural education.* Boston: Allyn & Bacon.

Bennett, C. (1989). *Preservice multicultural teacher education: Predictors of student readiness.* Paper presented at the annual meeting of the American Educational Research Association, San Francisco. (ERIC Document Reproduction Service No. ED 308161)

Bliss, I. (1990). Intercultural education and the professional knowledge of teachers. *European Journal of Teacher Education, 13*(3), 141-151.

Brown, S. C., & Kysilka, M. L. (1994). In search of multicultural and global education in real classrooms. *Journal of Curriculum and Supervision, 9*(3), 313-316.

Clandinin, D. J., & Connelly, F. M. (1992). Teacher as curriculum maker. In P. W. Jackson (Ed.), *Handbook of research on curriculum* (pp. 363-401). New York: Macmillan.

Collins, R. L. (1993). Responding to cultural diversity in our schools. In L. A. Castenell, Jr., & W. F. Pinar (Eds.), *Understanding curriculum as racial text: Representations of identity and differences in education* (pp. 195-208). Albany: State University of New York.

Estrada, K., & McLaren, P. (1993). A dialogue on multiculturalism and democratic culture. *Educational Researcher, 22*(3), 27-33.

Garcia, J., & Pugh, S. L. (1992). Multicultural education in teacher preparation programs: A political or an educational concept? *Phi Delta Kappan, 74*(3), 214-219.

Gollnick, D. M. (1992a). Multicultural education: Policies and practices in teacher education. In C. A. Grant (Ed.), *Research and multicultural education: From the margins to the mainstream* (pp. 218-239). London: Falmer.

Gollnick, D. M. (1992b). Understanding the dynamics of race, class, and gender. In M. E. Dilworth (Ed.), *Diversity in teacher education: New expectations* (pp. 63-78). San Francisco: Jossey-Bass.

Goodwin, A. L. (1994). Making the transition from self to other: What do preservice teachers really think about multicultural education? *Journal of Teacher Education, 45*(2), 119-131.

Grant, C. A., & Secada, W. G. (1990). Preparing teachers for diversity. In W. R. Houston (Ed.), *Handbook of research on teacher education* (pp. 403-422). New York: Macmillan.

Haberman, M., & Post, L. (1990). Cooperating teachers' perceptions of the goals of multicultural education. *Action in Teacher Education, 12*(3), 31-35.

Irvine, J. J. (1992). Making teacher education culturally responsive. In M. E. Dilworth (Ed.), *Diversity in teacher education: New expectations* (pp. 79-92). San Francisco: Jossey-Bass.

Martin, R. E. (1991). The power to empower: Multicultural education for student-teachers. In C. E. Sleeter (Ed.), *Empowerment through multicultural education* (pp. 287-297). Albany: State University of New York Press.

Mason, R. (1987). Helping student teachers broaden their conception of art curricula. *Art Education, 39*(4), 46-51.

McCarthy, C. (1994). Multicultural discourse and curriculum reform: A critical perspective. *Educational Theory, 44*(1), 81-98.

McDaniel, C.O., Jr., McDaniel, N. C., & McDaniel, A. K. (1988). Transferability of multicultural education from training to practice. *International Journal of Intercultural Relations, 12*(1), 19-33.

McDiarmid, G. W., & Price, J. (1990). *Prospective teachers' views of diverse learners: A study of the participants in the ABCD project.* E. Lansing: Michigan State

University, National Center for Research on Teacher Education. (ERIC Document Reproduction Service No. ED 324308)

Nel, J. (1992). Pre-service teacher resistance to diversity: Need to reconsider instructional methodologies. *Journal of Instructional Psychology, 19*(1), 23-27.

Peshkin, A. (1992). The relationship between culture and curriculum: A many fitting thing. In P. W. Jackson (Ed.), *Handbook of research on curriculum* (pp. 248-267). New York: Macmillan.

Ramsey, P. G., Vold, E. B., & Williams, L. R. (1989). *Multicultural education: A source book.* New York: Garland.

Rios, F. A. (1991). *Teachers' implicit theories of multicultural classrooms.* Unpublished doctoral dissertation, University of Wisconsin, Madison.

Sleeter, C. E. (1991). Introduction: Multicultural education and empowerment. In C. E. Sleeter (Ed.), *Empowerment through multicultural education* (pp. 1-23). Albany: State University of New York Press.

Spears, J. D., Oliver, J. P., & Maes, S. C. (1990). *Accommodating change and diversity: Multicultural practices in rural schools.* Manhattan: Kansas State University, Rural Clearinghouse for Lifelong Education and Development.

Tran, M. T., Young, R. L., & DiLella, J. D. (1994). Multicultural education courses and the student teacher: Eliminating stereotypical attitudes in our ethnically diverse classrooms. *Journal of Teacher Education, 45*(3), 183-189.

Tyson, H. (1994). *Who will teach the children: Progress and resistance in teacher education.* San Francisco: Jossey-Bass.

Vavrus, M. (1994). A critical analysis of multicultural education infusion during student teaching. *Action in Teacher Education, 16*(3), 47-58.

Walker, D. (1990). *Fundamentals of curriculum.* San Diego, CA: Harcourt Brace Jovanovich.

Watkins, W. H. (1991). Social reconstructionist approach. In A. Lewy (Ed.), *The international encyclopedia of curriculum* (pp. 32-35). Oxford: Pergamon.

Watkins, W. H. (1994). Multicultural education: Toward a historical and political inquiry. *Educational Theory, 44*(1), 99-117.

Weber, M. (1978). *Economy and society* (Vol. 1; G. Roth & C. Wittch, Eds.). Berkeley: University of California Press.

Zeichner, K. M. (1993). Connecting genuine teacher development to the struggle for social justice. *Journal of Education for Teaching, 19*(1), 5-20.

Zimpher, N. L., & Ashburn, E. A. (1992). Countering parochialism in teacher candidates. In M. E. Dilworth (Ed.), *Diversity in teacher education: New expectations* (pp. 40-62). San Francisco: Jossey-Bass.

Prospective Teachers Constructing Their Own Knowledge in Multicultural Education

- *Sharon Adelman Reyes*
- *Nayda Capella-Santana*
- *Lena Licón Khisty*

All of the classes I have taken up to this point in my college career have filled my head with facts and formulas . . . my classes have not emotionally moved me in any way, until now. This class has affected my life. I have changed my feelings as well as my mind about what kind of person and teacher I want to be. (P-1)

These are the words of a European American prospective teacher reflecting on her recent experience as a participant in a required course in multicultural education. Her words are similar to those expressed by many of her peers enrolled in the same class. These prospective teachers entered the course because it was part of the required curriculum for certification; some felt angry or even hostile to have had this enrollment forced on them. Yet the power that a uniquely and carefully designed multicultural education course can have on prospective teachers' professional and personal development is evident on listening to their voices. The purpose of this chapter is to describe this course and to offer an example of reconceptualizing a college classroom to better foster sense-making and cognitive change.

In the following sections, we will discuss first the theoretical basis for the course design and then, how the course was implemented. Throughout the chapter, we will let the participants speak for themselves by way of examples from their informal dialogue writing. The teachers' voices will be indicated by the letter "P" for "prospective teacher" with an identifying number. These prospective teachers were enrolled in a junior-level course as part of a teacher preparation program in a large, urban university. The enrollment included one Asian American male and 31 females, about a third of whom were Latinas and one who was Arabic. The majority of the participants, of course, were European American. However, although the composition of the class may seem atypical given the relatively substantial number of minority prospective teachers, as will be seen, the concepts presented here applied equally well to all prospective teachers.

■ Background

A course in multicultural education has become commonplace in teacher preparation programs around the country. Frequently, such a course is the only one that a prospective teacher is required to take to gain an understanding of diversity, particularly as it relates to schooling processes. It is here where prospective teachers must come face to face with the very likely possibility that a third of their future students will not be like themselves (National Center for Education Statistics, 1992) and that their assumptions about students cannot be taken for granted. Even the few minority prospective teachers who enter the profession cannot assume that their ethnic or racial status qualifies them to effectively reach all the diverse students they may have in their classrooms; minority teachers also "may have had minimal contact with people different from themselves as well and/or look on others with disdain" (Boyle-Baise & Grant, 1992, p. 189).

The increasing diversity in the nation's student population, coupled with the fact that the overwhelming majority of new teachers still are European American (e.g., Grant & Secada, 1990), makes the multicultural education course a critical element in working toward a teaching and learning process that is much more linguistically and culturally responsive and thereby, more effective for students who are also often educationally at-risk. However, these courses have not always been successful in positively affecting prospective teachers' attitudes toward cultural diversity (e.g., Ahlquist, 1991).

■ The Theoretical Framework

Why have such well-intentioned efforts not always met with the desired results? Our hypothesis was that traditional approaches to teaching any university-level course, in this case multicultural education, involves prospective teachers learning in a way that keeps knowledge outside of themselves. The typical learning situation, even with some of the most innovative strategies, still is too often structured around the objective that the student adopt some formal knowledge that has already been constructed by someone else. In light of this, a course on multicultural education is vulnerable to being seen by students as just another activity to take up time. Furthermore, the structure lends itself to creating or reinforcing stereotypes because students are learning what someone else (be it the instructor or writers in the field) has constructed in generalized terms about diverse groups. Consequently, the structure of the learning situation may actually be counterproductive to the intentions of multicultural education.

As an alternative, it was assumed that the participants had access to formal knowledge of multicultural education in the form of a textbook that in essence is a reference. What had to be created was an environment that fostered a transformation of the external formal knowledge into something much more meaningful. The course had to aim toward more personal intellectual growth rather than toward content growth. In fact, Banks (1993) has suggested that the area of multicultural education most in need of work pertains to the "construction of knowledge process"; the curriculum needs to be "reconceptualized to help students understand how knowledge is constructed and how it reflects human interests, ideology, and experiences of people who create it" (p. 37).

The course, therefore, was based on the idea of using personal learning experiences that paralleled the introduction of concepts of multicultural education. The intention was to maximize participants' seeing multicultural education as something emanating from themselves. It was assumed that once a person had placed multicultural concepts within her or his own life, the knowledge constructed by the self could be used as a bridge to understanding a perspective outside of the self. Therefore, the course focused on the following ideas:

- Having participants recognize that their own lived reality is multicultural education itself

- Defining diversity as opening channels of communication between participants

- Incorporating the experiences participants bring as a way of valuing and validating the human activity

- Having participants critically analyze their own experiences to reinforce the concept of the construction of knowledge

- Developing participants' sense of self as cultural researchers by conducting ethnographic ministudies

Critical to this process was the implementation of what Fernandez-Balboa and Marshall (1994) call "dialogical pedagogy." Within this perspective, serious dialogue between and among *all* members of the class served both for cognitive change and for transforming social relations within the classroom, thus raising awareness about relations in the broader society. Ultimately, the intention was to model what Banks (1993) calls *equity pedagogy* and thereby, to model the kind of teaching we hope teachers will actually engage in, teaching that is based on the idea that knowledge is something that is constructed from their own students and hopefully, that is more democratic by implication.

With this in mind, questions by the instructor were deliberately designed to spur thinking, analysis, inquiry, and debate (Fosnot, 1989). Because all participants were given maximum opportunity for meaningful input, more questions were constantly being generated as part of the input, and these questions in turn sparked class activities. Thus, the particular class activities were a natural outgrowth of, and dependent on, participants' input and questions. In this sense, specific activities were less instrumental in shaping course content and outcomes than the dialogue that created them. As doors were opened for students to influence or even to create the curriculum, horizons for exploring cultural diversity widened.

■ Broadening the Multicultural Framework

In keeping with the ideas just described that guided the course, if participants were to use their own experiences to understand multicultural education, then the framework of the subject had to be broadened to provide opportunity to incorporate these experiences. In this section, we will describe how this was accomplished.

Gender Diversity

Multicultural education is too often framed in terms of Black versus White issues. Such a narrow focus inherently eliminates all other groups (e.g., women and language minorities) and inadvertently fosters a sense of "we" versus "them." Chow (1993) also advocates for more inclusiveness when she argues that "the concept of feminism needs to be broadly defined to address the interconnectedness of sex, gender, race, class, and culture so that its defining character and meaning are grounded in the experience of various kinds of women" (p. 217). A parallel view for the course was adopted: The content of multicultural education was expanded to include as central the issues of language diversity and gender as well as the traditional issues of race, class, and culture. Such an approach encourages deeper personal and cognitive acceptance because it can more closely place central issues within the actual experiences of the individual.

Therefore, gender was a major concept to be discussed because all participants but one were female. Gender, like race, is socially constructed; gender hierarchies, like racial hierarchies, are manifested in our social institutions and demand considerations of equity. Elementary schools are no exceptions, for it is in the early grades that gender role expectations are often developed and reinforced (e.g., O'Reilly & Borman, 1984).

It was found that prospective teachers were highly reflective on gender as it related to the overall concept of equity. One Latina participant offered the following:

> Ever since . . . we have talked about the differences in treatment of males and females in society, I just find myself thinking about it in every situation I'm in. . . . The other day, I was at my uncle's house . . . [for] a barbecue. . . . There were five men and four women altogether. The men were . . . drinking, eating, and talking while the women were by the grill taking care of the food. It angered me that all the men were in their own little crowd, so I told my aunt . . . I would turn the meat so she could . . . join the men. . . . I came across another incident just the other day. . . . It is so upsetting to me that these things go on, but at the same time, you're dealing with your whole family and what is now tradition to them. I feel that we do have to start making our girls have more self-esteem starting in school. We need to make sure there is no gender bias in our classroom. . . . Ever since I have been taking this class . . . I have to admit

I don't think any topic in my education classes had ever struck me as hard as this one to be interfering with my personal life. (P-2)

The issue of gender roles continued to hit home and emerge even when discussing other concepts. For example, the words of another Latina participant illustrate the difficulty she encountered in expressing her new voice in front of male family members:

Something really great happened to me on that week that we had the Native American speaker. We went over to some friends' house, and I was amazed to hear that a much older man was talking very stereotypically about Native Americans. . . . This got my blood boiling, and I didn't care if he was an older man or that my husband and my father were there listening to his nonsense. I told him that I totally disagreed with him. . . . I was afraid my father or my husband would tell me to be quiet, but they didn't. My father smiled at me and winked. (P-3)

What is striking in listening to these passages is that in both instances, the prospective teacher recognized a concept discussed in class playing itself out in her own life. In each case, class reading and dialogue proved powerful enough to motivate action in the realm of personal experience.

An unexpected outcome of grounding the course content in lived realities was the request by one particular participant to discuss the topic of homosexuality within the discussion of gender. Initially, this concept had not even been thought of for inclusion in the course. However, here is an example where the student's understanding of the concept of diversity was the spark not only for other participants' construction of knowledge but also for that of the instructor.

Many participants expressed initial surprise that the concept of diversity in education could pertain to lesbian and gay students. To enhance this understanding, a self-identified lesbian guest speaker was invited to the class to participate in class dialogue on this subject. Judging from participants' responses, the impact of this session was significant. As illustrated by the following sample from participant-written comments, minority and European American participants both came away with new knowledge, insights, and perspectives.

I . . . realized . . . that I am more naive than I ever thought. . . . Before [our guest speaker] came to speak to our class, I did not know that there was a large population of gay adolescents. I thought only adults could be homosexual. It never occurred to me that those adults may have been homosexuals as teens. (P-4)

As can be seen in the previous writing excerpts, gender role expectations and hierarchies are topics too often overlooked in the general teacher education program; however, these concepts play themselves out in actual elementary and secondary school classrooms. These issues lend themselves to dialogic discussion within a multicultural education course and to enhancing understanding of equity. A focused theoretical and grounded look at feminism, along with the concept of "compulsory heterosexuality," hold the potential to deepen prospective teachers' understandings of the role of gender in the elementary classroom.

Language Diversity

Just as gender was an excellent vehicle for understanding diversity because it could be grounded in the experiences of the largely female group, so too, was language diversity because one third of the same group came from homes where English was not the only language spoken. However, it should be noted that language diversity and the concurrent issues of learning in two languages were part of the content, not simply because the participants "could relate to it" but because it is a critical concept in multicultural education.

Within the last 15 years, there has been a radical shift in the demographic profile of American schools. For example, the population of Spanish-affiliated language minority students (LMS) increased nearly 50% (Armstrong, 1991). Yet the institutional change in response to this has been minimal. The severest shortage of certified teachers is in bilingual education (Milk, Mercado, & Sapiens, 1992). This shortage, coupled with the growing LMS population, suggests that a significant portion of LMS spend their entire school day in classrooms with teachers who have little or no knowledge of, much less skills in, creating effective multilingual learning environments. In light of this, it becomes evident that *all* teachers need fundamental knowledge and skills on effective instruction for LMS (e.g., Khisty & Hernandez, 1992; Milk et al., 1992). A natural starting place is in a multicultural education course with key concepts being revisited and elaborated in later general or bilingual specialization courses. The power of ongoing and sustained dialogue on the topic of language diversity was reflected over and over again in prospective teachers' writings. Here is one example:

> Before I began [this class], I believed the best way to teach children a new language was to place them into a classroom in which only the new language was spoken. . . . I had heard success stories that supported this theory of "submersion.". . . . I asked one of my "success stories" how he really felt about being placed in a class in which he did not know the language that was spoken. Although . . . he learned the new language, my friend told me he felt left out, lost most of the time, and quite uncomfortable. I realize now that there are alternate programs that are fair to the student and to the teacher. (P-4)

This is the voice of a European American monolingual prospective teacher. However, the issue of language diversity had a strong impact on prospective teachers of color as well. A Latina participant wrote,

> My dilemma is that I fear that my children may not know or want to know Spanish. . . . I strongly feel that I will search for a school that offers a [Spanish] Immersion Program or one that attempts to have both Spanish and English spoken in the school. . . . This class has made me seriously consider being a bilingual teacher. (P-9)

As can be seen by the preceding example, the process of grounding the concepts of language diversity in lived realities can influence university-level LMS to consider the possibility of becoming bilingual teachers. With the projected shortage of certified bilingual education teachers and the escalating numbers of LMS in schools, that is no small accomplishment.

Thus far, we have suggested that a prerequisite for constructing knowledge is the ability to relate personally to the concept. Having various experiences and perspectives in a class, that are used as the basis for learning, allow participants to relate to a wide range of issues. For example, many of the women in the course were able to relate personally to issues of gender; many of the Latina and Asian participants, as well as the one Arabic participant, were able to relate in the same manner to the issues of language diversity. A deeper sense of understanding can occur when these connections are made. Furthermore, the questions and issues we discussed came not only out of texts and research studies but out of our collective examination of our lived realities. As one prospective teacher wrote, "I think the most advantageous part of the whole course was hearing real-life examples of teaching experiences and classroom situations" (P-4).

■ Broadening the Multicultural Course Context

Multicultural education is generally taught from a textbook and in a classroom. In designing this course, however, we wanted to move the context of learning beyond the classroom and to capitalize on the community around us. We wanted participants to become inquiring teachers and to think of themselves as anthropologists doing cultural studies in relevant neighborhoods and community institutions. The intent was to make concrete to a greater extent the topics we had been talking about.

The ministudies emerged as a result of class dialogue in which participants generated an array of questions and ideas about the nature of diverse communities. In essence, participants were to do investigations as scientists do them (Warren, Rosebery, & Conant, 1989), by posing their own questions, designing their own investigations for getting answers to these questions, and defending their data and conclusions. For example, several European American participants wondered if they would be welcomed as educators in a low-income, African American community. They decided to find the answer in a concrete way by attending an event in such a setting.

Although these were ministudies and not intended to generate elaborate investigations, the approach was intended to amplify participants' sense of constructing their own knowledge. Furthermore, it was hoped that this experience would serve other functions. First, as a result of going beyond the classroom, participants would discover through concrete activities and tangible experiences that ethnic and racial communities were not as culturally and intellectually limited as is often assumed. In the beginning, the experience was guided in such a way that participants would perceive seemingly poor neighborhoods as rich in what Moll and his colleagues (e.g., Moll & Greenberg, 1992) call "funds of knowledge." Participants were asked to explore communities for what they could offer as educational resources and possibilities for study—for example, what kids do after school for sports, arts, and extended learning. Second, participants would begin to build a base of community knowledge that could enhance their understanding of their students and their families and thus facilitate their abilities to genuinely use their students' experiences. Thus, their self-initiated investigations took them to social service centers, museums, and public school meetings. Third, participants could begin to form relationships with community members that could enhance their personal and professional growth regarding cultural diversity. Because many participants chose to do their investigations in the same or similar communities to those in which they later would do their student teaching, it was hoped that the relationships forged as a result of the ministudies would directly link personal and professional growth. Last, this experience could foster redefinition of the role of teacher to include cultural and community researcher.

The anthropological ministudies provided an opportunity for European American participants to get substantially different and positive perspectives on environments often characterized negatively. One such participant was overwhelmed by the positive reception she received from African American parents in the city's notorious "Westside," where she attended a community meeting. Unable to contain her excitement, she seized the next class period to share information and literature she had obtained from that experience.

Ministudies such as these have been discussed by Tran, Young, and DiLella (1994) who found that "cultural plunges," where "students immerse themselves in a cultural activity and interact with members of another culture [are successful in creating] an intimate link between schools and their community" (p. 188). Let the following participant voice the power of cultural immersion:

> I enjoyed this class because I learned more than just theories and studies. . . . I gained knowledge of the many diverse communities that exist in Chicago, something that I will definitely need and take with me when I begin teaching in the public school system. (P-7)

In addition to taking the classroom into the community, the community was brought into the classroom. Six people who represented a wide variety of communities and who were strongly active in those settings were invited to attend separate class sessions and to discuss what learning resources they saw in their communities. The words of a Latina student reflect many of the comments expressed by class participants in regard to redefining the community as a "fund of knowledge":

> I am glad that a connection to the communities was made in the beginning of the class. . . . Hearing the guest speakers represented from

the many diverse communities in Chicago has given me a true meaning of multicultural education. Learning about the community resources, from the site visits taken by the whole class, has also made a strong connection to multicultural education. The guest speakers and site visits had an overwhelming impact on me. (P-7)

■ Conclusions and Discussion

Within the last two decades, research on issues of equity and the interactions among race, class, ethnicity, gender, and schooling outcomes has provided a rich knowledge base for the content of multicultural education courses. What is still at issue is how to create a cognitive change in teachers so that this knowledge base is effectively used to bring about educational reform. The premise of the present discussion has been that changing the teaching and learning process for university students who are preparing to be teachers can result in more substantial cognitive changes, particularly with regard to diversity. As an opportunity to test this hypothesis, the course we have described yielded many insights into the nature of these changes.

Prospective Teacher Attitudes

Individuals who once failed to see the importance of a linguistically and culturally sensitive and responsive curriculum and classroom environment can come to better understand the nature of such concepts in practice. The words of a European American prospective teacher are representative of many of the reflections of class participants on completion of a semester of study:

During my weeks and months in this class, I've done a lot of reflecting and growing. I think back to my old views, and I feel as if I was walking around with blinders, like most people. When it came to multicultural education, I thought including ethnic names in story problems, having books with ethnic names, and having ethnic parties did the trick. Being a future teacher, I can not believe I thought that way! (P-10)

Other participants commented on how their new insights had already affected the manner in which they were preparing for their future students. Another European American participant wrote,

Recently, in the preparation of a project for another education course, I was required to develop a week-long unit using several children's literature books to create a theme. . . . I thought that my theme would be all about multiculturalism. Well, as proof of my constant reflection in this area, I realized that this method of teaching would not be wonderful after all. I would in fact be separating these issues from the rest of the curriculum. (P-6)

A change was also noted in how teachers of color viewed their future roles. The words of a Latina participant are particularly moving. The following passage clearly illustrates the necessity of challenging the teacher belief systems of prospective teachers of all racial, ethnic, and linguistic backgrounds:

I now know and understand the importance of providing multicultural education for all students, not only the minorities. . . . I also learned the reason why so many of us minorities are not successful in the schools. I have to confess that I believed, like many other people, that the reason for this was that we didn't try hard. I thought that we were to blame for our failure. . . . Never did it cross my mind to think that the reason for our failure is that we live in a racist society, which infiltrates our school systems that perpetuate the social system instead of trying to destroy it. It is sad to see that such inequalities like the practice of tracking still exist. (P-3)

Personal Beliefs and Practices

In addition to affecting attitudes on teaching, individuals can learn to reexamine personal beliefs and practices regarding issues of gender, race, language, and ethnicity that in turn may affect their developing teaching styles.

One evening, I was doing some homework, and my younger brother was watching the television show *Fresh Prince*. . . . During this particular episode, Fresh Prince is talking with his sister. He asks her a question, and she replies, "Sí, señor." Then he says, "You've been hanging out with the gardeners again?" Well, I really found this offensive. For the first time in my life, I felt something. It was really powerful! I asked my brother what he thought of the statement, and he said, "So what. What's the big deal?" I had an answer! It all came together for me. More importantly, I realized that the purpose of this class for me was to be able to say that things like these comments are a big deal. (P-1)

As these words of this European American prospective teacher indicate, constructing one's own knowledge of cultural diversity can effect a reexamination of beliefs and practices also related to the world outside of the classroom. A strongly grounded knowledge of cultural diversity may be instrumental in developing a new way of viewing the world. In the words of another prospective teacher,

It is because of this class that . . . I now carefully watch television commercials, department store advertisements, who is covered in the news and newspaper and how they are covered. I meticulously dissect television sitcoms, hunting for their hidden messages. I only hope I maintain this sensitivity when I no longer meet with a group that reinforces these activities. (P-12)

A Voice of Advocacy

Prospective teachers who understand the importance of respect for diversity but have not always had the words to express their position can find the voice to do so. Again, this finding holds for both minority and European American prospective teachers. For the final paper, one Latina participant wrote a play inspired by her recent conversations with peers from other campus courses and activities. In her prologue, she wrote,

I am expanding in my answers [to them] using knowledge from what I have learned in [this class]. The idea being that if I were able to return in time, my knowledge acquired from [this class] would help me to better challenge people's forms of thinking. (P-13)

In the same vein, a European American participant wrote,

At the beginning of the semester, I would have never been able to defend anything I've said about discrimination or stereotypes other than the fact that it's wrong. Now, I feel as if I could get into a lengthy debate on why teachers and people in general need to open up their minds to the world. (P-14)

These comments suggest that when prospective teachers are engaged in constructing their own knowledge of cultural diversity, multicultural education can have an impact that goes beyond the classroom. The voices of culturally empowered teachers hold the possibility of causing others, both inside and outside of the teaching profession, to critically examine their personal and professional beliefs in regard to diversity. These are voices that need to be let loose and heard.

A Dialogical, Process-Oriented Pedagogy

Because our pedagogy included setting a norm in which questions were constantly investigated rather than answered by a text, participants learned that it was acceptable, even desirable, to pose questions that could not be immediately answered. In this regard, we found that asking questions could be stimulating rather than threatening and facilitative rather than limiting of dialogue. In fact, what emerged was the realization (particularly for the instructors) that questions from both participants and teachers had a spiraling effect on what happened in class. As participants talked, questions arose that in turn generated inquiries that generated more questions and created more dialogue. We discovered that the learning process could have no end when approached dialogically, that interactive learning builds on and facilitates further learning, and that the process generates its own excitement and serves as a motivating source that keeps the learning fresh.

We also have learned first hand that the burden of "good teaching" does not lie in the activity but in the process, and the process is embedded in dialogue. The issue for the teacher becomes posing the right question at the right time to foster the dialogue.

Given the nature of our discussion, we feel compelled to make note of an unanticipated outcome related to the dialogic process. Just as caution is needed to avoid generalizing about minority students, we discovered that the same caution is needed with regards to all groups, including European Americans. This realization came about because our own assumptions of European American teachers were challenged. At first glance, the class seemed typical of prospective teachers in its homogeneity. It is interesting that by shifting from a pedagogy that emphasized passiveness and listening to one that actively engaged students and drew on their own experiences, we discovered the rich medley of student lives that actually existed. For example, a number of European American prospective teachers did not fit the stereotypes associated with this group. One woman came from a home with a European American mother and an African American stepfather and lived in an African American community. Another woman was a mother of two who lived in a low-income Latino community and found her children uniquely situated as European American minorities in their neighborhood school. Two other participants had strong Jewish cultural identities and additionally viewed themselves as members of a religious minority. Others represented personal experiences with single parenthood and learning disabilities.

■ Some Final Thoughts

Did the course accomplish what it intended? Can we see positive change in the ways prospective teachers view and think about implementing multicultural education? We cannot claim to answer this question conclusively; the final test will come in these prospective teachers' own future classrooms. Yet we cannot dispel the power of their own voices. Although a great deal of thought went into thinking about how to foster participants' construction of their knowledge, we have to acknowledge that we did not expect the intensity with which the participants responded. In the same vein, we did not expect students to write statements like, "This class has affected my life." We did not expect to hear about them challenging family members and family traditions in positive ways. Neither did we expect participants to readily identify that they had not seen a whole picture and that their knowledge had been limited. Through these and other comments, we are able to see a clear difference in attitudes before and at the conclusion of the course. There appears to be adequate information to suggest that internalization has begun. How far it will go, we cannot say. We are hopeful, however, that it is the beginning of a lifelong process.

■ References

Ahlquist, R. (1991). Position and imposition: Power relations in a multicultural foundations class. *Journal of Negro Education, 60*(2), 158-170.

Armstrong, L. (1991, March 1). Census confirms remarkable shifts in ethnic make-up. *Education Week*, p. 1.

Banks, J. A. (1993). Multicultural education: Historical development, patterns, and practice. In L. Darling-Hammond (Ed.), *Review of research in education 19* (pp. 3-49). Washington, DC: American Educational Research Association.

Boyle-Baise, M., & Grant, C. A. (1992). Multicultural teacher education: A proposal for change. In H. C. Waxman, J. Walker de Felix, J. E. Anderson, & H. Prentice Baptiste (Eds.), *Students at risk in at-risk schools* (pp. 174-193). Newbury Park, CA: Corwin.

Chow, E. N. (1993). The feminist movement: Where are all the Asian American women? In A. M. Jaggar & P. S. Rothenberg (Eds.), *Feminist frameworks: Alternative theoretical accounts of the relations between women and men* (pp. 212-219). New York: McGraw-Hill.

Fernandez-Balboa, J., & Marshall, J. P. (1994). Dialogical pedagogy in teacher education: Toward an education for democracy. *Journal of Teacher Education, 45*(3), 172-182.

Fosnot, C. T. (1989). *Inquiring teachers, inquiring learners: A constructivist approach for teaching.* New York: Teachers College Press.

Grant, C. A., & Secada, W. G. (1990). Preparing teachers for diversity. In W. R. Houston (Ed.), *Handbook of research on teacher education* (pp. 403-422). New York: Macmillan.

Khisty, L. L., & Hernandez, J. (1992). *Reconceptualizing staff development for bilingual education.* Paper presented at the AERA Annual Conference, San Francisco.

Milk, R., Mercado, C., & Sapiens, A. (1992). *Rethinking the education of teachers of language minority children: Developing reflective teachers for changing schools.* Washington, DC: National Clearinghouse for Bilingual Education.

Moll, L., & Greenberg, J. B. (1992). Creating zones of possibilities: Combining social contexts for instruction. In L. C. Moll (Ed.), *Vygotsky and education: Instructional implications and applications of sociohistorical psychology* (pp. 319-349). New York: Cambridge University Press.

National Center for Education Statistics. (1992). *Digest of education statistics.* Washington, DC: Government Printing Office.

O'Reilly, P., & Borman, K. (1984). Sexism and sex discrimination in education. *Theory Into Practice, 23*(2), 110-116.

Tran, M. T., Young, R. L., & DiLella, J. D. (1994). Multicultural courses and the student teacher: Eliminating stereotypical attitudes in our ethnically diverse classroom. *Journal of Teacher Education, 45*(3), 183-189.

Warren, B., Rosebery, A. S., & Conant, F. R. (1989). *Cheche Konnen: Science and literacy in language minority classrooms* (BBN Technical Report No. 7305). Cambridge, MA: Bolt, Beranek, & Newman.

PART III

Culturally Literate Teachers

Preparation for 21st Century Schools

- *Claudette Merrell Ligons*
- *Luis A. Rosado*
- *W. Robert Houston*

The United States is often called a nation of immigrants. The United States is really the world in microcosm because it represents such a broad cross-section of peoples throughout the world community. *The*

AUTHORS' NOTE: The restructured teacher preparation program at the four participating universities was recognized as "The Distinguished Program in Teacher Education" at the 76th National Conference of the Association of Teacher Educators, February 28, 1996, in St. Louis, MO. The following three researchers have contributed to this chapter: Dr. Judith Walker de Felix, Professor and Associate Vice Provost for Faculty Affairs at the University of Houston, contributed from her research in bilingual teacher education and classroom processes; Dr. Linda Roff, Professor and Director of the Center for Professional Development and Technology at Houston Baptist University, contributed from her research in teaching strategies and multicultural education; Dr. Higinia Torres-Karna, Associate Professor and Director of the Title VII Program in the School of Education at the University of St. Thomas, contributed from research in bilingualism and second-language acquisition.

Harvard Encyclopedia of American Ethnic Groups (Themstrom, Orlov, & Handlin, 1980) identified more than 500 distinct ethnic groups in our country. A broad cross-section of these ethnic groups has contributed to the nation's advancement. Still, the value of ethnic and cultural diversity is not widely shared in the broader society nor in the education community. Some see diversity as an asset, whereas others see it as a liability, and the way we see diversity colors our response to it.

Research findings (Darder, 1991; Escalante & Dirman, 1990; Grant & Sleeter, 1994; Hilliard, 1991; Ligons, 1992) have established that educators' responses to ethnic diversity have a direct effect on students' academic performances. Teacher expectations are shaped, in part, by student ethnicity and income, thereby influencing how they teach (Brophy, 1983; Ralph, 1989). This information has powerful implications for the ongoing professional development of teacher educators and for all other major stakeholders in the preparation of the nation's teachers.

This chapter will (a) present a novel consortium of institutions that pooled resources to create a new framework for preparing teachers to serve urban learners, (b) examine the perceptions of one preservice teacher regarding culture and schooling, and (c) present a sampling of institutional experiences and activities that were designed to develop culturally literate teachers.

■ A Novel Consortium of Institutions

Research findings on the relationship between learner performance and teacher response to diversity are of special significance to the Consortium of Urban Professional Development and Technology Centers, in one Texas metropolis. The Consortium's mission is the preparation of teachers who will be especially equipped to produce academic success among urban learners. The Consortium, a state-funded initiative, is composed of two education support centers; 16 professional development schools; and four area universities, two of which are private and two of which are state supported.

The professional development schools in the Consortium were selected to reflect the widest range of ethnic and socioeconomic conditions in the city. For instance, students in one school are virtually all Hispanic, with a large proportion of students who lack proficiency in English. Another school is almost entirely African American, with families that represent a range of socioeconomic backgrounds. Another school is balanced ethnically, with roughly one-fourth Asian, one-fourth African American, one-fourth Hispanic, and one-fourth European American students.

Fifteen Consortium outcomes frame the evolving teacher preparation programs. One of the most important outcomes is that preservice teachers demonstrate cultural literacy and responsiveness: the capacity to interact comfortably with persons from various ethnic and cultural groups and the ability to make culturally based instructional and curricular adaptations that enhance students' opportunities to succeed. The changing ethnic demographics in Texas make cultural literacy of teachers particularly important. A 1994 report from the Texas Education Agency (TEA) showed that although almost 52% of Texas students are from ethnic groups of color, some 77% of Texas teachers are from European American ethnic groups. The underrepresentation of teachers from ethnic groups of color in Texas is consistent with trends across the nation. This discrepancy indicates an imperative to equip all teachers with the relational and instructional competence to produce academic success among students from various ethnic backgrounds (TEA, 1994).

The Consortium focus on preparation of teachers for urban learners will ensure that beginning teachers function at a higher level of confidence, comfort, and competence in urban settings. Although the 15 Consortium outcomes were developed in 1991-1992, they are consistent with the five broad proficiencies for teachers presented in *Learner-Centered Schools for Texas: A Vision of Texas Educators* (TEA, 1995). On February 7, 1997, The State Board of Educator Certification approved these proficiencies as the Standards for the Preparation of Texas Educators— Learner-Centered Proficiencies for Teachers, Administrators, and Counselors. These standards are congruent with those of the National Council for Accreditation of Teacher Education (NCATE) and the Interstate New Teacher Assessment and Support Consortium (INTASC) of the Council of Chief State School Officers. Last, INTASC's standards were developed in line with the performance standards of the National Board for Professional Teaching Standards (Gollnick, 1994). These standards are intended to upgrade the performance of teachers all along the spectrum, including preservice preparation, beginning licensure, renewable licensure, and board certification. Two of INTASC's expected competencies for new teachers are the "understanding and use of instructional opportunities for culturally diverse and exceptional populations" and "planning and managing instruction based on knowledge of the content areas, the community, and curriculum goals" (Gollnick, 1994, p. 7).

A Preservice Teacher's Perceptions
of Culture and Schooling

The imperative to develop teacher cultural literacy is dramatically illustrated in the following log entry. It was written by a preservice teacher.

> Why be concerned about culture? After all, we live in the same country. Most of us speak the same language, and those who don't, have a chance to learn English in school. Most of us dress the same, bathe every day, and enjoy the same foods and entertainment and comforts. If you don't think so, just spend some time in a really foreign country. Then, you'll see just how American you are. Sure, I plan to be a teacher and I see it as my responsibility to help everyone learn to the best of their ability and to fit into the American society. When we start to look at differences between races and other groups, we tend to develop stronger stereotypes. Besides, I think it's prejudiced to look at a person's race or cultural differences, especially in the classroom where we're supposed to treat everyone equally. (Bennett, 1995, p. 2)

What he believes is fairly common among persons who have not become culturally literate. It demonstrates the need for the development of essential affective and cognitive teacher competencies that equip teachers to support the academic success of a broad cross-section of students in the nation's schools.

There are some troubling assumptions in this preservice teacher's statement. These are the key assumptions: (a) As a nation, we are culturally homogeneous; (b) students' lack of English proficiency is a matter of choice; (c) the school assumes a major role in the socialization of students; and (d) a color-blind attitude is evidence that one is ethnically and culturally unbiased. This preservice teacher is not atypical. An analysis of his beliefs about culture and schooling dramatically demonstrate the need for culturally framed teacher preparation and professional development.

Assumption of Cultural Homogeneity

The preservice teacher assumes that because we live in the same country, we are culturally alike—that there are no discernible differences among us. He makes an effort to support this assumption with his suggestion that living in another country would magnify those commonalities. To some degree, elements of core U.S. culture are more apparent when compared and contrasted with elements of core culture in another country. However, living in another country can also make our differences more apparent. For instance, there are differences in both verbal and nonverbal patterns of communication among various ethnic communities in our country. Sometimes, the failure to act on these differences contributes to the misunderstandings in cross-ethnic communication.

Assumption Regarding Lack of English Proficiency

Most citizens in the United States speak English though not all speak "school English." Also, there are many different languages spoken in the homes of school-age children. For instance, in one large school district in Texas, the 1993-1994 school profile identified more than 60 languages spoken in the homes of students. In Texas, bilingual programs are designed primarily for students whose home language is Spanish, and the programs function almost exclusively at the elementary school level. Therefore, the opportunity for developing English language fluency is drastically reduced for limited English proficient (LEP) students entering school after the elementary school years and for students whose home language is other than Spanish. This practice makes a first language other than English a liability rather than an asset, often resulting in remediation and the concomitant lower expectations for LEP and bilingual students. This perception is common despite research evidence on the value of binguality.

In a classic study conducted in 1962 on the relationship of bilingualism and cognitive processing, Peal and Lambert (as cited in Nañez, Padilla, & López Maez, 1992) found that bilingualism appeared to enhance intelligence and cognitive flexibility among bilingual Canadian children. In other research, Nañez, Padilla, and López Maez (1992) analyzed 30 studies that were conducted between 1921 and 1987. They found that of the 10 studies conducted between 1962 and 1987, all reported a positive correlation between binguality and cognitive processing. This dual language asset is not widely recognized in the broader community nor in the schools. Therefore, it is not nurtured and promoted in the school community.

Assumption Regarding the School's Role in Socialization

The preservice teacher assumes a responsibility to shape students' behavior to help them fit into U.S. society. For the culturally literate teacher, that shaping and fitting involves a delicate balance between helping students to assimilate elements of core U.S. culture while at the same time retaining elements of their home culture. One-way cultural shaping is assimilation. Assimilation has been shown to result in a loss of core cultural identity, particularly for students from ethnic groups of color. When socialization demonstrates regard for the home culture, the process enlarges students' cultural world rather than shrinking it by erasing elements of the foundational home culture. This is an additive rather than a subtractive approach, and it demonstrates a culturally friendly response to diversity.

Assumption of Evidence That One Is Unbiased

The last assumption is that one can be color-blind, and that this is synonymous with being culturally responsive. First of all, humans are not ethnically color-blind. Color and ethnic differences are visible, and they help define who we are. Acknowledging a person's ethnic or racial group membership only becomes negative if negative meaning is assigned to the observation. When ethnic difference is acknowledged in positive ways that do not demean, there is no reason why teachers should pretend that they do not see these differences (Ayers, 1988). A color-blind attitude that results in teachers using the same instructional and motivational strategies for *all* students can produce inequitable patterns of learner performance. Ignoring ethnic difference when there are instructional or relational implications can contribute to student underperformance. On the other hand, focusing exclusively on differences will not create a basis for genuine relationships across ethnic and cultural groups. Relationships within and across groups require some common ground on which to build.

Like others, the preservice teacher who made this entry in his log expects to become a good teacher. However, his performance as a teacher would be greatly enhanced with a clearer understanding of the relationship between culture and schooling. These are not two separate universes. Virtually all of the human experience is housed in culture—in language; humor; thinking styles; learning styles; and in political, economic, and spiritual values. Therefore, culture cannot be ignored in the education enterprise if we are committed to the highest quality of education for all (Gay, 1992; Haberman, 1996).

The development of culturally literate teachers focuses on cultural differences that directly affect learning. This requires accommodation for learner differences that include information processing styles, communication styles, and learning styles. To some extent, each of these style differences is culturally derived (Castaneda & Gray, 1974; Hale, 1982). Accommodating these style differences reduces the burden on learners to adjust to the requirements imposed by the school. Ideally, teachers make these adaptations for differences while retaining high regard for students' ability to perform. This thinking represents a striking contrast to the perception that instructional adaptations must be made because of student deficits. The culturally literate teacher makes modifications to accommodate student differences, not deficits. The Consortium institutions address equity issues in the preparation of teachers. The increased attention to teacher cultural literacy is consistent with Standards for NCATE, the INTASC, and the State Board of Educator Certification in Texas.

■ Institutional Experiences That Promote Cultural Literacy

The major stakeholders in the Urban Consortium are engaged in restructuring the four teacher preparation programs that function as the centerpiece of Consortium activities. The end goal is to improve the performance of students in urban schools in particular. The framing principles of the school models that have proven successful with urban learners have been studied in this process. This creates a research base for the evolving program changes.

The Consortium links a pool of talent from all of the collaborating institutions. What is common among the evolving teacher preparation programs is a commitment to create a new generation of urban teachers by merging best teaching practices with leading-edge technology. Differences in the universities' missions have led to differences in the approaches being tested to achieve the overarching goal.

The following information is a sampling of approaches on which initial field tests have been conducted and includes multicultural policies, practices, and experiences across the consortium institutions. The approaches use both simulated and real-world experiences to sharpen preservice teachers' responsiveness to the links between culture and schooling. The multicultural teaching competencies are an integral part of the preparation program. Therefore, the multicultural experiences are embedded in the warp and woof of the professional development courses and selected methodology courses.

Consortium members establish the value of intercultural literacy early in the admissions process, which includes a formal interview and a portfolio to determine prospective teachers' readiness in four broad areas. These are (a) academic background, (b) language proficiency, (c) cross-cultural experiences, and (d) genuine commitment to teaching. The admission process has evolved from gatekeeping to a diagnostic procedure for prospective teachers. Therefore, prospective teachers can be admitted conditionally if they have no evidence of successful cross-cultural interactions. They work with their instructors to build the expertise, necessary knowledge, skills, and attitudes to support their success in urban classrooms. Though some protest the conditional admission, most begin to value cultural proficiency. This is evident in their requests for more information about children's cultures, home experiences, values, and learning styles once they begin working with the children on a regular basis. The cultural diversity in the professional development schools in the Consortium provides extensive opportunities for preservice teachers to develop cross-cultural interaction skills.

A second way in which the Consortium has integrated cultural perspectives is through program advisement. Preservice teachers are encouraged to gain the English as a Second Language endorsement to enhance their teaching effectiveness with language minority students. However, these powerful teaching strategies enhance teacher performance with all students.

Third, prospective teachers may adopt and tutor a school-age child for a designated time frame. Prospective teachers are encouraged to choose a student from an ethnic and cultural group that is different from their own.

Similarly, prospective teachers can elect to shadow a child who is linguistically different and make notes on how curricular resources and instruction would be changed to more effectively accommodate the linguistic diversity.

Consortium members also expect the preservice teachers to document successful experiences communicating with members of various ethnic and cultural groups in Texas schools as well as with students who are cognitively and physically challenged.

Prospective teachers in the Consortium must demonstrate their commitment to teaching and to high performance expectations for all youth. The documentation includes a portfolio of experiences and three letters of recommendation. Portfolios are used to supplement traditional assessment measures (Tellez, Walker de Felix, & Palmer, 1994).

Another of the guiding principles in the teacher preparation programs is that university students will learn to be effective teachers in urban schools if they learn the framing principles and associated content both experientially and theoretically. Therefore, the university instructors are expected to model the instructional and interactional teacher behaviors that foster urban students' success.

The first portfolio is assembled after a student has observed all teachers in the professional development school, taught lessons to small groups, and served as teacher assistant or teacher aide.

Portfolio assessment is a major component of the programs because authentic instruction requires authentic assessment. Portfolios require students to assemble evidence of milestones they have reached. This allows students from diverse backgrounds to use their own voices and products to make the case for their learning. With experience, the faculty has learned to guide students in the use of the "value added" principle in assembling evidence of proficiency. That is, they were instructed not to add evidence that did not increase the value of the portfolio. This dispelled the notion that a bigger portfolio is better.

The final portfolios are presented when the university students complete student teaching. The intent is to demonstrate that they are "safe to start" teaching. One of the former students found the issues of cross-cultural interaction the most compelling, including communicating with families of different ethnic groups, observing conflict among teachers of different backgrounds, and working with a teacher who seemed indifferent to multicultural principles. Students learn from both positive and negative example, though we prefer the former.

To guide the preservice teachers to become more inclusive in their thinking, Consortium members engage their students in games and simulations to broaden their thinking. One example is Bafa Bafa (an intercultural interaction game that enhances cultural responsiveness). Also, preservice teachers become more responsive to a broad cross-section of students as they participate in simulations that focus on characteristics of academically gifted students and students with learning disabilities.

School placement sites are critically important to Consortium members. Ethnically isolated communities are common in many urban metropolitan areas. By selecting different school settings—largely Hispanic, African American, largely European American, and one that is ethnically balanced—prospective teachers experience settings that may be different from those where they went to school but very similar to those where they will teach.

Numerous multicultural scholars have described schools as academic islands where many teachers commute to in the morning then escape as soon as possible in the afternoons. To help preservice teachers understand the organic nature of the school within the community, pre-

service teachers conduct a study of the community immediately surrounding the school, including social service agencies and area businesses, to gain a more comprehensive view of their students' lives beyond the school.

Consortium members also encourage the preservice teachers to be
active with parents' education. In one instance, preservice teachers conducted an after-hours computer training program for stay-at-home,
Spanish-speaking mothers. The training was voluntary, and the students conducted the training entirely in Spanish in the afternoons. Baby-
sitting was provided for the mothers who had young children.

Preservice teachers also established an electronic pen pal program
that paired their students with university students from diverse ethnic
backgrounds who served as role models. The school-aged students
gained access to computer technology and telecommunications not or-
dinarily found in the regular classroom.

Last, Consortium members also use traditional classroom approaches to increase cultural responsiveness and instructional accountability. For example, preservice teachers participate in seminars that
build their skills in cross-cultural communication. One of the major tenets of the Consortium is the emphasis on reflective inquiry. As students
work in school, they are encouraged to reflect on their experiences, particularly the differentiated reactions of students to classroom encoun-
ters. At the end of each week, students reflect on their experiences during the week, seeking a deeper understanding of what they have seen
and heard. These classes have often been videotaped, so the group could
examine at leisure what they could not do in the heat of classroom interaction. Nuances of dress, psychological distance, and language and its
influence on students are part of the discussions that occur.

Prospective teachers have had discussions of their experiences in
school and in university-based seminars for years; this practice is not
new. What is new is the reflection and the analysis based on technologi-
cal re-creation of the situation. What is new is the emphasis on individual students, their actions and interactions, their facial expressions and
other nonverbal behaviors, particularly during instruction or periods of
unstructured activities.

Some events are deliberately videotaped for analysis. For instance,
an African American prospective teacher who was working with Hispanic middle school students was concerned with the interaction between the third of the class who were African American and the half who
were Hispanic. She videotaped their interactions during a free period
and again at lunch. Then, she interviewed them to determine their per-

ceptions of school, their classmates, and their hopes and desires for the future. She also completed three sociographs—one related to their social desires ("Who would you like to spend the weekend with you?"), their athletic ability ("Who would you choose to be on your team?"), and their academic perceptions ("Who would you choose to be in your group to complete a project in social studies?"). From these data, three sociographs were constructed and analyzed. The most intriguing aspects were found when ethnicity and gender were superimposed on the graphs. Data from the sociographs were used as basic information for a group of prospective teachers to view the videotapes, consider results of interviews, and develop a more realistic view of cross-cultural interaction.

Consortium stakeholders recognize that prospective teachers are not born with innate abilities to spot the nuances related to gender; they must be taught about the research and theoretical constructs that undergird diversity and its manifestations in classroom interactions. Furthermore, they need to have contact with students from diverse backgrounds and to experience differences and respond to them. Last, small groups need to work together so their perceptions are sharpened by the ideas of others. The varied experiences that have been presented are intended to enhance the entry-level performance of first year teachers in urban schools. Our attention to culture in the preparation of teachers also confirms our belief that teaching excellence is the delicate balance between instructional and interactional competence.

The success of beginning teachers during their initial 3 years is a major factor in their decisions to continue their assignments in urban classrooms. Preliminary research data are reported in the following section on the effectiveness of the restructured teacher preparation programs.

■ Promising Program Results

Do these activities make a difference? During the past 3 years, we have engaged in extensive studies of the various components of the program and their impacts on both our students and prekindergarten to 12th grade (PK-12) students. Surveys were conducted of the perceptions of teachers in the programs' 16 professional development schools, university faculty, and students. Here are the five major findings:

1. Prospective teachers in these programs teach differently from those in more traditional programs. Two sets of student teachers were observed during the 1995 spring semester, using a signed observation instrument. Prospective teachers in this program interacted more often with PK-12 students in their classes and in more personal ways than those in a comparison group. They spent significantly more time in (a) responding to students' signals, (b) checking students' work, (c) encouraging self-management, (d) praising student behavior, (e) praising student performance, and (f) correcting student performance. In a survey, 78% of their cooperating teachers indicated that they believed the performance of preservice teachers had changed as a result of the new program.

2. Teachers in the 16 professional development schools teach differently. An independent survey was conducted in the spring of 1995 to determine the extent to which the program had influenced practices and programs in professional development schools; 42.9% of teachers indicated that they had changed how they taught based on information and skills acquired through participation in the program's activities. Nearly three fourths (74.2%) had participated in one or more of the program's professional development activities.

3. University faculty teach differently when they are teaching classes in schools. They can present a concept, have their students observe or tutor or teach, then discuss its nuances and implications. The community context and the individual nuances of students' backgrounds and knowledge can be used as concrete bases for theoretical constructs.

4. The professional knowledge of preservice teachers tends to be greater than in traditional programs. Texas requires teacher preparation students to pass a test of professional knowledge (ExCET) at the end of their preparation program as a prerequisite to certification. A greater proportion of preservice teachers in this program passed the ExCET on the first attempt than students in traditional programs (range of 92%-100% as compared to 58%-85% on the various tests). Because many of the questions in the professional development test focus on application, the increased time that preservice teachers spent in schools and the emphasis on personal attributes of students may have contributed to differences in achievement.

5. Student achievement in public schools tended to increase after the schools became professional development schools. Students in Texas schools are required to take the Texas Assessment of Academic Skills in three areas. When achievement in 1994-1995 was compared with that of 1992-

1993 (prior to participation in the program), the percentage of students passing mathematics increased in all 16 professional development schools. Achievement in reading increased in 14 of 16 schools and in 10 of 16 schools in writing. It is interesting that prospective teachers tutored and worked with small groups in mathematics and reading but not in writing. All professional development schools were engaged in activities to improve the achievement of their students, thus this finding is contaminated with other interventions; however, the pattern of change is interesting and encouraging. These early findings suggest that both ordinary and extraordinary teachers, who are committed to teaching excellence, can contribute significantly to the academic success of urban learners.

■ References

Ayers, W. (1988). Young children and the problem of the color line. *Democracy and Education, 3*(1), 20-26.

Bennett, C. (1995). *Comprehensive multicultural education theory and practice* (3rd ed.). Boston: Allyn & Bacon.

Brophy, J. (1983). Research on the self-fulfilling prophecy and teacher expectations. *Journal of Educational Psychology, 75*(5), 631-661.

Castaneda, A., & Gray, T. (1974, December). Bicognitive processes in multicultural education. *Educational Leadership, 32*(3), 203-207.

Darder, A. (1991). *Culture and power in the classroom.* New York: Bergin & Garvey.

Escalante, J., & Dirman, J. (1990, Summer). The Jaime Escalante math program. *Journal of Negro Education, 59*(3), 407-423.

Gay, G. (1992). Effective teaching practices for multicultural classrooms. In C. Diaz (Ed.), *Multicultural education for the 21st century* (pp. 38-56). Washington, DC: National Education Association.

Gollnick, D. (1994). New accreditation standards: Focus on performance. *NCATE Quality Teaching, The Newsletter of the National Council for Accreditation of Teacher Education,* p. 7.

Grant, C., & Sleeter, C. (1994). *Making choices for multicultural education: Five approaches to race, class, and gender.* New York: Macmillan.

Haberman, M. (1996). Selecting and preparing culturally competent teachers for urban schools. In J. Sikola (Ed.), *Handbook of Research on Teacher Education* (2nd ed., chap. 32). New York: Macmillan.

Hale, J. (1982). *Black children: Their roots, culture, and learning styles.* Provo, Utah: Brigham Young University Press.

Hilliard, A. (1991, September). Do we have the will to educate all children? *Educational Leadership, 49*(1) 31-36.

Ligons, C. (1992). Producing high academic yields in urban schools: Philoso-phies, policies, and practices. *Texas Southern University Research Journal 3*(1), 71-97.

Nañez, J., Padilla, V., & López Maez, B. (1992). Bilinguality, intelligence, and cognitive processing. In R. V. Padilla & A. H. Benavides (Eds.), *Critical per-spectives on bilingual education research* (pp. 42-69). Temple, AZ: Bilingual Press.

Ralph, J. (1989, January). Improving education for the disadvantaged: Do we know whom to help? *Phi Delta Kappan, 70*(5), 395-401.

Tellez, K., Walker de Felix, J., & Palmer, A. (1994, April). *Multiculturalizing teacher education in urban professional development schools.* Paper presented at the American Educational Research Association, New Orleans, LA.

Texas Education Agency. (1994, May). *Texas teacher diversity and recruitment* (Re-port No. 4.). Austin, TX: Author, Office of Policy Planning and Evaluation.

Texas Education Agency. (1995, October). *Learner-centered schools for Texas: A vi-sion of Texas educators.* Austin, TX: Author, Publications Distribution Office.

Thernstrom, S., Orlov, A., & Handlin, O. (1980). *Harvard encyclopedia of American ethnic groups.* Cambridge, MA: The Belknap Press of Harvard University Press.

What Difference Does Preparation Make?

Educating Preservice Teachers for Learner Diversity

- *Andrea Guillaume*
- *Carmen Zuniga*
- *Ivy Yee*

Institutions of teacher education have rushed to address the needs of the swelling numbers of students who speak languages other than English and whose cultures are other than the U.S. mainstream. For example, California has recently mandated more thorough preparation for new teachers in meeting the needs of culturally and linguistically diverse learners through its Crosscultural, Language, and Academic Development (CLAD) and Bilingual Crosscultural, Language, and Academic Development (BCLAD) credentialing requirements.

The diversification of the student population, and the changes in teacher preparation necessitated by it, give rise to a number of concerns. Just as the nation's student population diversifies, its teaching force becomes more homogeneous (Canella & Reiff, 1994). Teachers may view students through their own "cultural prism." They may not be ready to understand or address the learning needs of their students. In California, for example, although in 1996, 1.3 million students were classified as English learners, only 13,500 teachers held bilingual credentials. This equates to about one bilingual teacher for about 100 students. In addition, 25% of these 1.3 million students received no English language instruction at all (California Department of Education, 1996). In addition to the inability of many states to meet students' immediate language needs, it is also difficult to prepare adequate numbers of qualified teachers in the longer range. This is because, among other reasons, the number of practicing teachers who can serve as appropriate role models is small and because university faculty themselves often need to upgrade their own skills in culturally and linguistically inclusive instruction. Last, even when preparation programs are in place and operating, lasting effects of new, mandated efforts to prepare teachers to meet the needs of diverse learners have yet to be carefully assessed. The study discussed in this chapter addressed the problem of the uncertain effects of teacher preparation efforts for learner diversity by asking, "What difference does preparation make?"

■ The Literature

A growing body of literature points to the critical need for teachers who successfully address the learning needs of students of diverse backgrounds (Banks & McGee Banks, 1995; Garcia, 1993; Merino & Faltis, 1993). Similarly, the literature gives many recommendations and suggestions on ways to improve teacher preparation programs to help novice teachers meet learning needs of these students (Banks, 1993; Garcia & Pugh, 1992; Kestner, 1994). Isolated success stories are provided through case studies of individuals or small groups of teachers or school sites (Lucas, Henze, & Donato, 1990; Milk, 1994; Zuniga-Hill & Yopp, 1996). Yet we continue to be dismayed by statistics revealing that minority students fare poorly in schools across the nation. Teachers and teacher educators continue to find it difficult to penetrate a monocultural perspective of how to teach.

Why do we continue to struggle with ways to improve educational success for students of color? One reason is that teacher beliefs are quite rigid and resistant to change (Pajares, 1992). Pajares stated that, "beliefs are far more influential than knowledge in determining how individuals organize and define tasks and problems and are stronger predictors of behavior" (p. 311). He further suggested that individuals acquire belief systems through cultural transmission, that new knowledge is filtered through one's belief system, and that the earlier a belief is incorporated, the more resistant to change it is. Thus, it is not surprising that teachers' practice does not change easily.

Numerous examples in the literature document teachers' apparent inability or resistance to engage in effective teaching for students of color. Mata and Jordan (1994) described an extensive Clinical Supervision Initiative examining conditions affecting the quality of field supervision practices of university supervisors and cooperating teachers. Student teachers in this study, their cooperating teachers, and the university supervisors all independently agreed on the most-growth and the least-growth areas during the field experience. One of the four of the least-growth areas was working with limited-English and non-English-proficient students, despite student teachers' being placed for at least one semester of field work in a multicultural setting.

Ahlquist (1991) and Avery and Walker (1993) also found that preservice teachers carry with them attitudes and beliefs that do not predispose them to successfully teach students of color. So did Dilworth (as cited in Kestner, 1994), who described an incident wherein an African American student displayed a keen knowledge of dialect usage in a piece of her writing, but her teacher appeared unable to value or appreciate the student's writing. According to Kestner, situations like this will recur until teachers can engage in instruction that is sensitive to and inclusive of diversity.

Kestner (1994) recommended several approaches for improving professional preparation for diverse teaching contexts. Indeed, the literature suggests that cases can be used to help access teachers' reasoning and beliefs and hold promise for furthering teachers' growth (Kagan, 1993). In sum, the literature indicates the dire importance of improving teachers' attitudes and abilities for working with diverse groups of learners, and such work is difficult given the intractable nature of teachers' belief and knowledge systems. Thus, it is important not to assume that professional training practices are having the desired effect in encouraging growth for prospective teachers and to continue to explore models that do promote growth.

■ Method

Background

The authors are engaged in an ongoing research program to assess and improve their efforts to prepare teachers to encourage learning for all students. In a first study (Guillaume, Zuniga-Hill, & Yee, 1994), the authors asked three groups of preservice teachers to respond to a classroom case. These groups included

1. a beginning group with no student teaching experience and extremely limited preparation for diversity,
2. an experienced group whose classroom experiences afforded them some exposure to diverse groups and whose university instruction included some instruction in linguistically and culturally responsive pedagogy, and
3. an experienced group who student taught in highly diverse settings (often where they delivered instruction in a language other than English) and received systematic university instruction in culture and language.

Despite differences in their preparation, these groups responded to the case with approximately the same degree and sophistication of attention to diversity issues. That is, when essay responses were holistically scored for attention to diverse learners' needs, a comparison of the groups' mean scores resulted in nonsignificant differences. Variations in the extent and kind of preparation participants received were not reflected in their written responses to a case in learner diversity, and the majority of participants in each of the three groups responded to diversity issues in limited, superficial ways.

Since that study was conducted, the authors' institution enhanced its preparation program by (a) adding a CLAD/BCLAD program (designed to provide earlier and more extensive university course work and field experiences for encouraging learning for students of color) to its training options and (b) bolstering its instruction for diversity by modifying its instructional focus. Instructional changes primarily include asking students to examine their own perspectives and experience diversity issues as learners themselves. An example is the extended use of other-than-English language lessons that model effective meaning-making techniques and strategies. After these lessons, students examine their emotional responses to instruction and articulate what especially helped them make sense of the lessons. Students engage in a simulation lesson called "Gibberish" that impedes communication between two groups and sets up empowered and powerless relations among the students. They also read vignettes and then respond from an affective perspective to the effects of prejudice and inappropriate schooling experiences. For example, students are asked to respond both on a personal level and as teachers to a story of a Lebanese child who was ridiculed by other children. The child ran home and lamented to her grandmother,

---

"Why do they do it?" Hoda sobbed. "Don't they know that it is all I have? *Indee isin. Hatha kul ma indee.* I have a name and nothing more. I don't have blue eyes. I don't have money. I don't have a big house. I don't speak English. All I have is my name, and when they laugh at my name, they laugh at me and all that I am. And it hurts. I want to go way. I want to go home, away from here, far far away."

"Hush, my darling," Grandma whispered . . . "your name means 'gift' and to us you will always be a beautiful gift." (Mundahl, 1993, p. 17)

As instructors, we hoped that these instructional changes would be reflected in preservice teachers' treatment of diversity issues.

The Current Study

As was the aim of the authors' earlier study, the purpose of the current study was to explore prospective teachers' responses to a case in learner diversity. However, two important modifications were made. First, a new group of participants from the CLAD-BCLAD program was added. These participants' preparation for working with diverse learners was even more thorough than was that of participants in the first study. Second, in the first study, participants received no prompting for learner diversity as they composed their essays. In the current study, participants composed essays, then participated in focused small-group discussions centering on issues of learner diversity. Such discussions might allow tacitly held notions of learner diversity to surface, and they might enrich participants' answers by exposing participants to varying viewpoints. CLAD-BCLAD participants composed a second set of essays after participating in discussion.

Participants' two sets of essays were holistically scored and subjected to two comparisons. First, the prediscussion essay scores of the CLAD-BCLAD were compared to those of a group of less thoroughly prepared preservice teachers. Second, prediscussion and postdiscussion essay scores for the CLAD-BCLAD group were compared to determine change in treatment of diversity issues brought about by the discussion.

Participants

Both groups of participants—CLAD-BCLAD and the less thoroughly prepared group—were enrolled in a fifth-year elementary certification program at a large public university in an ethnically rich area of California. The first of these two groups of participants consisted of 48 student teachers near the end of their credentialing program. These preservice teachers were primarily white, female, and monolingual. They received one semester unit of instruction in modifying curriculum and instruction to meet the needs of culturally and linguistically diverse students. One of their two semesters of student teaching was required to be in a setting where at least 25% of the children were identified as minorities.

The second group of participants ($n = 26$) was part of the new CLAD-BCLAD program. These preservice teachers elected to pursue special certification for working with students with diverse backgrounds. They had completed a three-unit prerequisite course in multicultural education in the classroom in addition to a three-unit course focused on modifying curriculum and instruction for second-language learners. About one fourth of these participants had learned English as their second language, and the remaining participants had completed at least six semester units of a second language requirement. Though Spanish was the most frequently occurring other language, some participants spoke Vietnamese or Korean. Furthermore, they student taught in situations where the master teacher was certified to work with diverse groups.

Instruments

Instruments include the classroom case, the essay prompts, and the holistic scoring rubric.

The Classroom Case

The case of Marsha Warren (Silverman, Welty, & Lyon, 1992) was selected by Rudney and Guillaume (1994) because it was realistically complex in presenting issues of diversity intertwined with numerous other classroom issues. In this actual case, Marsha was driven to frustration by her third graders who interfered with her ability-grouped, basal-text reading lesson. Though Marsha noted that her students were heterogeneous in terms of cultural heritage, English proficiency, reading level, and academic ability, her explanation of their misbehavior was that the class was, overall, immature. Marsha became so frustrated by her students' disruptive behavior—especially by that of the heterogeneous students in the lowest reading group, the "infidels"—that she shouted at the class and left for the silence of the hall. The case closed as Marsha, after analyzing her students and the modifications she had attempted to date, stood ready to reenter the room.

The Essay Prompts

Both groups of participants responded to the case by addressing three prompts:

1. What are the issues in this case?
2. What would you do if you were Marsha?
3. What might be the consequences of your actions?

These prompts were designed to be open-ended so that issues of diversity might surface but so might other issues, such as classroom management, theories of reading instruction, and professional support. Thus, participants could respond to the case by identifying the issues most striking to them.

After responding to these three prompts, the second group of participants (CLAD-BCLAD) also responded to another set of prompts, first in small-group discussion, then in writing.

1. Are there issues of culture and language in this case?
2. If yes, what would you do if you were Marsha?
3. What might be the consequences of your actions?

The Scoring Rubric

In response to the conceptual and empirical literature that suggests that teachers of diverse students need to develop a knowledge base about ethnic groups, use instructional strategies that make learning available for all students, and serve as advocates for their students of color by evidencing a firm commitment to understanding the children's world view and to furthering their students' and their own learning (reviewed in Guillaume, Zuniga-Hill, & Yee, 1994), the authors developed a five-point rubric. Summarized, scores were assigned by the rubric as follows:

0: No explicit treatment of cultural or linguistic diversity.

1: Brief mention of diversity issues, but no strategies presented to address those issues. Single words.

2: Recognition and treatment of diversity issues but in superficial ways. Teacher-centered response. Unrelated strategies.

3: Consideration of children's world view. Teacher recognizes shared responsibility for student learning. Evidence of knowledge base. Related strategies.

4: Items from 3, and strategies integrated into an overall approach; knowledge base is extensive, recognition of hierarchy of needs; questions accepted practices; recognition of the need for growth in one's own attitudes, knowledge, behaviors.

Procedure

During separate administrations, both groups of participants read the case silently, then responded in writing to the essay prompts. Because the authors no longer retained access to this group, participation for the first group ended at this point. However, after submitting their essays, the second (CLAD-BCLAD) group of participants engaged in 15 minutes of small-group discussion, focused by the second set of prompts, given earlier. At the close of their discussions, participants individually composed a new set of essays in response to these prompts.

■ Analysis

Each prediscussion essay was blindly read and then scored by the three authors. In every case, the authors' scores were adjacent or in exact agreement. These sets of prediscussion essays were compared using a one-way, fixed-effects Analysis of Variance. Essays with scores of 0 (no explicit treatment of diversity issues) were excluded from the ANOVA.

TABLE 9.1   Descriptive Statistics by Group

	Group 1 *(Less Thoroughly Prepared)*	*Group 2* *(CLAD-BCLAD)*
Proportion of essays with score of 0 (no treatment of diversity issues)	30 of 48 (63%)	5 of 27 (19%)
Mean scores of essays scored 1 to 4	1.9	1.6
Mode of essays scored 1 to 4	2	1
Minimum, maximum scores	1, 4	1, 4
Standard deviation	0.74	1.06

The second group of essays, the postdiscussion set completed by the CLAD-BCLAD participants, was also read and scored blindly by the three authors, using the same rubric. The prediscussion and postdiscussion essays of this group of participants were compared using a t-test for dependent means.

To explore participants' reasoning in greater depth, the essays were also qualitatively analyzed. One author took primary responsibility for examining themes found throughout the essays. The two other authors challenged and refined those themes through supporting analyses.

■ Results

Results support the findings of the authors' earlier study and other works in the literature (e.g., Mata & Jordan, 1994; Pajares, 1992) that suggest it is difficult to promote change in teachers' reasoning related to diversity issues. Findings are explored by examining comparisons of the groups and by examining comparisons before and after focused discussion.

Comparisons of the Groups

Table 9.1, which gives descriptive statistics for both groups, indicates that two thirds of the essays composed by Group 1 (the non-CLAD-

BCLAD group) did not address issues of diversity, whereas only one fifth of Group 2's essays neglected to address issues of diversity. However, those essays that did address diversity issues in the two groups did so with a similar degree of depth.

Zero responses, more prevalent for the less thoroughly prepared teachers, often centered on issues of classroom management. For example, one student presented a list of issues:

Class management (behavior)

Can't grab the interest of the students

Low expectations

No support

Inconsistent

Rewards or acknowledges "bad" behavior more often than "good" behavior—negative reinforcement.

A score of 2, the modal score for Group 1, identified issues and then gave superficial treatment of them. The following is an example of a response at this level:

[Marsha had] a student named Jose who seemed to have developed BICS [basic interpersonal communication skills] but was lacking in CALP [cognitive and academic language proficiency]. His reaction was understandable. The teacher was unable to understand his frustration. There were also other students who were limited English proficient. The class was truly a mix of children from a variety of backgrounds. Before I would have lost it, I would have called in an observer. Marsha definitely needed a lot of help. She probably needed to use a school psychologist for some students and also get a bilingual aide. She needed to implement some cooperative learning into her class structure. Outcomes could be positive or negative depending on what Marsha did. Without help, she definitely was going to be in trouble with the school and the parents. With help, she had a chance of regaining respect for herself and the students, not to mention a higher success rate for the learning.

When the groups' mean scores were compared using a one-way analysis of variance, no significant difference between the two groups of participants' prediscussion essays was found ($F = 0.2, p > .65$). This indicates that, although participants who had more extensive university

TABLE 9.2   Group 2's Essay Scores Before and After Discussion

	Before Discussion	*After Discussion*
Mean score	1.29	1.93
Modal score	1.00	2.00
Minimum, maximum scores	0, 4	0, 3
Standard deviation	1.14	0.73

NOTE: Data include scores for all essays, including essays scored as 0.

preparation and classroom experience with diverse groups were more likely to treat diversity issues in their responses, they responded in no greater depth and evidenced no greater professional knowledge base than did those with more limited training and experience for working with students of color.

This finding coincides with findings from the first study in that differences in personal and professional preparation for working with diverse groups were not reflected in participants' essay responses to a case in learner diversity.

■ Comparisons of CLAD-BCLAD Groups' Essays Composed Before and After Discussion

Table 9.2 gives descriptive statistics for Group Two's (the CLAD-BCLAD participants) essay scores before and after discussion. This table indicates that the most frequently occurring score changed from 1 to 2 after discussion and that the range was narrower after discussion than it was before discussion. Five participants' essay scores declined after discussion, and 19 improved. However, a *t* test for dependent means indicate that the shift in means was nonsignificant ($t = -2.93$, tcrit, 2 tail = 2.05; $P(T < = t) = 0.00$).

Although this statistical test indicates that there was no significant improvement in scores as a result of discussion, qualitative analysis reveals some notable trends.

A closer examination of the data revealed that there were qualitative differences between the teachers who produced the following different types of responses: (a) essays with little or no difference between the scores of the prediscussion and postdiscussion responses, (b) prediscussion essays that had no mention of any issues of diversity but whose postdiscussion essays did offer limited, superficial treatment of the issues, and (c) postdiscussion essay responses that were scored lower than the prediscussion essay responses. A presentation of these differences by group as well as examples of these kinds of responses follows.

Scores That Exhibited Little Change After Discussion

Eight teachers gave virtually the same answer before and after the small-group discussion. In some cases, there was a bit more attention given to strategies employed to deal with the issues of diversity. For example, one teacher's prediscussion response stated this:

> Try to make activities fun for the group. Have meaningful reading in which the students can relate. Talk about culture in a lesson plan. Have them work in groups where they need their partner to succeed. Have a point system in which the students can gain points to acquire prizes. Reward for positive behavior. Call parents and discuss disruptive behavior of the child. Conference with parents, child, and principal. Investigate family problems. Be an authority figure at all times. Don't give up. Have high expectations versus low.

After the small-group discussion, the participant noted,

> I would have them work cooperatively. Work in pairs to help one another. I would also focus the readings on cultural topics. Topics that would interest them and perhaps be able to work and understand one another. The readings would definitely be meaningful and exciting to capture their attention. She would also need to stop using so many labels on the children. She needs to treat them as students who are capable of performing at higher levels. Not as slow learners. Have many visuals and hands-on materials. Have activities in which the students can interact and be a part of instead of just sitting and reading.

Scores That Improved Slightly After Discussion

A trend of moving from absolutely no mention of the issues of culture and language diversity to a listing of strategies intended to address such issues was shown by 12 participants. However, these responses also revealed that whatever had been the central focus of the respondent's prediscussion answer remained the central focus of his or her postdiscussion response. In some cases, expression of this focus was amplified, as though the treatment of the issues of diversity was an appended concern that did not replace earlier concerns. In addition, these essay responses revealed a clear focus on classroom management. Many of the respondents identified with the teacher, Marsha, but focused on her loss of control in the class. In many of the prediscussion essays, there were suggestions, including the implementation of alternative groupings, the use of positive reinforcement, and the development of the students' self-esteem. For example, one participant wrote that she would

> Praise the students who are doing their work and showing good behavior. Try not to focus and comment on the negative behaviors when they are minor ones. . . . Praising the good behavior turns attention of the class to the positive instead of the negative behavior."

Most of the participants retained this focus on classroom management in their postdiscussion essay responses but added on ways to address learner diversity.

> The students benefit from support and resources available to them. The students could manage their behavior in a more appropriate manner, and they could focus on the learning once they obtain strategies and help from outside sources.

The benefits of the focus discussion seem to be limited. Except for one case where scores changed from 0 to 3, the participants did not seem to qualitatively change their responses to reflect a shift in attitude regarding the source of the problems or the teacher's responsibilities for addressing those problems.

Scores That Declined After Discussion

The final group of essays included responses that showed a decrease in scores from prediscussion to postdiscussion. For three of the responses, this downward shift was not significant because their essays did not show notable qualitative changes. However, two participants whose prediscussion essays earned a score of 4 wrote postdiscussion essays that earned a score of 2 or 3. Closer examination of these two essays reveals that the prediscussion responses reflected the teachers' willingness to change their own attitudes to better meet the needs of their students:

I would need to investigate alternative methods of instruction, attend conferences, take classes, learn all I can in an attempt to discover other ways of reaching these children. . . . By educating myself, I would acquire knowledge of a variety of ways to approach situations and presenting of instruction of curriculum.

In contrast, postdiscussion responses contained a listing of strategies that did not reflect any of the personal investment evident in the prediscussion essay. Perhaps these two participants felt it unnecessary to restate their personal commitments, but it is also possible that the focus discussion had the effect of homogenizing the individual responses.

■ Discussion

The problem of bringing educational equity to life is complex and cannot be solved with simple solutions of isolated strategies, such as short-term workshops, a single university course or observation, or participation experience in a classroom with a diverse student population (Gomez, 1993). Bringing about the ability to examine issues from multiple perspectives and address them in satisfying, equitable ways is more than a matter of "punching one's multicultural ticket" (Garcia & Pugh, 1992, p. 216) through university instruction.

The essential question of how best to prepare teachers to work in diverse settings is not exclusively one of looking at teacher preparation in isolation. It must be placed in a larger context that examines an understanding of experiences, values, and beliefs that students and faculty bring to the teaching-learning situation (Baker, 1977; Cochran-Smith, 1996; Goodwin, 1994; Kuhlman & Vidal, 1993). This study's findings suggest that those participants (primarily the BCLAD candidates) who at least recognized issues of diversity in their written analyses brought with them personal experiences of having lived diversity and therefore, perhaps, the ability to assume the role of the "other." Teacher preparation may be most successful, then, when it is strongly linked to the diversity of human experiences and demands a personal examination of one's own values and recognition of sociopolitical realities and power relationships within our society (Garcia & Pugh, 1992).

Recognizing that appropriate responses to diversity seemed partly to depend on who participants were (rather than the training they received), how can teacher education begin to make inroads? It seems that a fundamental step would be to provide experiences that allow participants to broaden their base of cultural and linguistic sensitivities, not as teachers (a learned role) but as people (the fundamental role). Though valuable for all university students and faculty, exchange programs and travel may play a particularly crucial role in helping preservice teachers develop abilities to negotiate unfamiliar cultures and languages. As the teaching corps becomes increasingly homogeneous, the broadening of experiences of preservice teachers plays an even more important role.

Within the teacher preparation program, a starting point may be with preservice teachers' and faculty's own autobiographies. Life writings can reveal differences among experiences and surface attitudes and commitments to be fostered or further examined (Zulich, Bean, & Herrick, 1992).

Case studies, as a next step, may provide participants with an opportunity to examine how their life histories shape their analysis of classroom events. Case studies allow preservice teachers to "view any number of situations and to think about how to act, engage in dialogue concerning different approaches" (Kestner, 1994, p. 43). One important aspect about case studies—in print or on videotape or through multimedia presentations—is that they allow for shared discussion of a single set of classroom events from a number of viewpoints shaped by life histories and, we hope, by teacher preparation experiences. This study suggests that, although results were nonsignificant, a single 10-minute discussion of cases influenced the responses of many participants, primarily in terms of awareness of issues.

Brought outside the university classroom, newly surfaced knowledge of self, perspectives gained from peers, and knowledge gained through teacher preparation experiences can be carried into the schools for focused classroom observations of teachers who model appropriate approaches to issues of diversity. Interviews with these teachers can allow participants to probe for explanations and expand preservice teachers' observations and questions. Any strategy selected must be used with consideration of the larger goals of effecting change in well-formed belief systems and building commitments for helping all children learn.

■ References

Ahlquist, R. (1991). Position and imposition: Power relations in a multicultural foundations class. *Journal of Negro Education, 60*(2), 158-169.

Avery P., & Walker, C. (1993). Prospective teachers' perceptions of ethnic and gender differences in academic achievement. *Journal of Teacher Education, 44*(1), 27-37.

Baker, B. (1977). Multicultural training for student teachers. *Journal of Teacher Education*, pp. 306-307.

Banks, J. (1993). The canon debate, knowledge construction, and multicultural education. *Educational Researcher, 22*(5), 4-14.

Banks, J., & McGee Banks, C. (Eds.). (1995). *Handbook of research on multicultural education*. New York: Macmillan.

California Department of Education. (1996). *CBEDS, R-30 Language Census, Data/BICAL*. Reports 2A, 9C, 90-2. Author.

Canella, G., & Reiff, J. (1994). Preparing teachers for cultural diversity: Constructivist orientations. *Action in Teacher Education, 16*(3), 37-45.

Cochran-Smith, M. (1996). Color blindness and basket making are not the answers: Confronting the dilemmas of race, culture, and language diversity in teacher education. *American Educational Research Journal, 32*(3), 493-522.

Garcia, E. (1993). Language, culture and education. In Darling-Hammond, L. (Ed.), *Review of research in education* (pp. 51-96). Washington, DC: American Educational Research Association.

Garcia, J., & Pugh, S. (1992). Multicultural education in teacher preparation programs. *Phi Delta Kappan, 74*(3), 214-219.

Gomez, M. L. (1993). Prospective teacher's perspectives on teaching diverse children: A review with implications for teacher education and practice. *Journal of Negro Education, 62*(4), 459-474.

Goodwin, A. L. (1994). Making the transition from self to Other: What do preservice teachers really think about multicultural education? *Journal of Teacher Education, 45*(2), 119-131.

Guillaume, A., Zuniga-Hill, C., & Yee, I. (1994). Prospective teacher's use of diversity issues in a case study analysis. *Journal of Research and Development in Education, 28*(2), 69-78.

Hoffman, D. (1996). Culture and self in multicultural education. *American Educational Research Journal, 33*(3), 545-569.

Kagan, D. M. (1993). Contexts for the use of classroom cases. *American Educational Research Journal, 30*, 703-723.

Kestner, J. (1994). New teacher induction: Findings in the research and implications for minority groups. *Journal of Teacher Education, 45*(1), 39-45.

Kuhlman, N. A., & Vidal, J. (1993). Meeting the needs of LEP students through new teacher training: The case in California [Special issue]. *Journal of Educational Issues of Language Minority Students, 12*, 97-113.

Lucas, T., Henze, R., & Donato, R. (1990). Promoting the success of Latino language-minority students: An exploratory study of six high schools. *Harvard Educational Review, 60*, 315-340.

Mata, S., & Jordan, G. M. (1994, June). The induction of new teachers: The challenge of diversity. *Executive Summary*, pp. 18-21.

Merino, B., & Faltis. C. (1993). Language and culture in bilingual teacher education: Politics, research, and practice. In M. B. Arias & U. Casanova (Eds.), *Bilingual education: Politics, research and practice* (Vol. 92, pp. 171-195). Chicago: National Society for the Study of Education.

Milk, R. (1994). Responding successfully to cultural diversity in our schools: The teacher connection. In R. DeVillar, C. Faltis, & J. Cummins (Eds.), *Cultural diversity in schools: From rhetoric to practice* (pp. 144-169). Albany, NY: SUNY Press.

Mundahl, J. (1993). *Tales of courage, tales of dreams: A multicultural reader.* Reading, MA: Addison-Wesley.

Pajares, M. F. (1992). Teachers' beliefs and educational research: Cleaning up a messy construct. *Review of Educational Research, 62*(3), 307-322.

Rudney, G., & Guillaume, A. (1994, April). *An investigation of the relationship between case study analysis and student teaching performance.* Paper presented at the annual meeting of the American Educational Research Association, New Orleans, LA.

Silverman, R., Welty, W., & Lyon, S. (1992). *Case studies for teacher problem solving.* New York: McGraw-Hill.

Zulich, J., Bean, T. W., & Herrick, J. (1992). Charting stages of preservice teacher development and reflection in a multicultural community through dialogue journal analysis. *Teaching & Teacher Education, 8*(4), 345-360.

Zuniga-Hill, C., & Yopp, R. (1996). Practices of exemplary elementary school teachers of second language learners. *Teacher Education Quarterly, 23*(1), 83-98.

Pursuing the Possibilities of Passion

The Affective Domain of Multicultural Education

- *Francisco A. Rios*
- *Janet E. McDaniel*
- *Laura P. Stowell*

Many scholars in the field of multicultural-multilingual education have turned their attention to what can be done to effectively prepare teachers for the increasing cultural and linguistic diversity they are likely to encounter in classrooms (see, for example, the 1995 *Journal of Teacher Education, 46*(5) issue). These scholars have begun by documenting the knowledge and skills associated with exemplary teachers who are identified as competent in diverse linguistic contexts (Chu & Levy, 1988; Collier, 1985; National Association of State Directors of Teacher Education and Certification [NASDTEC], 1984) and diverse cultural contexts (Dwyer, 1991; Villegas, 1991). With respect to diverse language contexts, NASDTEC (1984) identified the following knowledge areas as being fundamental: the historical, philosophical, legal, and theoretical base associated with bilingual education; second-language acquisition; language structure and use; and sociolinguistics. They further suggest that teachers need to have the ability to implement instructional techniques (including English as a Second Language); to speak the students' native language; to communicate with students' parents in their community; to assess students; and to develop, implement, and evaluate practices in multilingual contexts.

With respect to effectiveness in culturally diverse contexts, Dwyer (1991) found that effective teachers have a solid content knowledge base, teach for student learning, create a "community" atmosphere in their classrooms, and advance themselves as professionals. Villegas (1991) added that these effective individuals teach in culturally responsive ways associated with, primarily, adapting to the learning style differences of their students.

Although much effort to prepare teachers for the increasing cultural and linguistic diversity of schools has been based theoretically on how individuals will move from self-awareness through awareness of others to teaching effectiveness (e.g., Locke, 1988), the actual empirical evidence to support the theory is less hopeful. McDiarmid and Price (1993) found that many prospective teachers' beliefs about diversity remained "untouched" even after a 2-year teacher education program. Other studies have expressed the fear that our multicultural efforts might actually have a negative effect, such as promoting stereotypes or trivializing the manifestations of culture (Garcia & Pugh, 1992; Martin & VanGunten, 1994; McDiarmid, 1992; McDiarmid & Price, 1993; Sleeter, 1992).

Two conclusions emerge from the studies just described. First, we have yet to find models of multicultural teacher education that work. Second, notable from the descriptors of effectiveness in culturally and linguistically diverse contexts is the lack of attention paid to affective considerations, even though one's disposition is as significant for student learning as are knowledge and skills (Darder, 1995; Erickson, 1987; Ladson-Billings, 1992; Pease-Alvarez, Espinoza, & Garcia, 1991; Rios & Whitehorse, 1994). For example, Erickson (1987) suggested that trust and personal relations were central for effectiveness in multicultural contexts. Ladson-Billings's (1992) review of the characteristics of a culturally responsive pedagogy included such elements as commitment to the students' community, teacher warmth, positive expectations, and a balance between task and relationship orientation. Darder's (1995) words hark strongly here when she argued for infusing education for diversity "with the possibilities of passion" (p. 328).

The notion of affect in education is not new. Krathwohl, Bloom, and Masia, in 1964, outlined what is described as the major categories in the affective domain of the taxonomy of educational objectives (Figure 10.1). In this description, individuals move from being willing to attend to (i.e.,

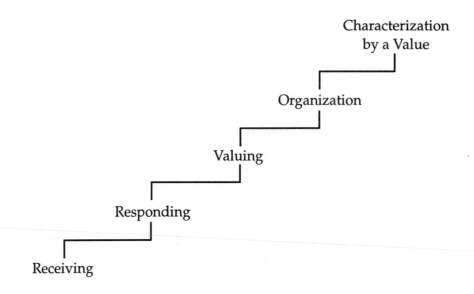

Figure 10.1. Krathwohl's Taxonomy for the Affective Domain
SOURCE: Adapted from Krathwohl et al. (1964).

receive) phenomena, to responding to them, to valuing them, to synthesizing them into their existing value schemes (i.e., organize), to characterizing themselves by the value or value complex. What has yet to be identified is a way in which this model might be adapted to explain how teachers come to value diversity.

This chapter presents a study of positive change in preservice student teachers' attitudes and knowledge at a university in Southern California. The first section identifies the context of the community, the university, the college of education, the middle level teacher education program, and the nature of the course in which the survey was administered. The second section describes the participants, methods, and procedures for analysis of the data obtained. The third section presents results. The last section discusses the results, proposes questions and challenges, and describes the implications for teacher education.

■ The Context

The University and Surrounding Community

California State University-San Marcos (CSUSM) was founded in 1989 and was the first university in the nation to be opened in a quarter of a century. The university is located between Los Angeles and San Diego, some 60 miles north of the United States-Mexico border. Despite its nearness to two major urban centers and the urban "tone" it is developing, San Marcos still has many of the characteristics of a rural agricultural community. The university campus was formerly a chicken ranch and was home to many migrant farm workers. The extended families of many of these migrant workers are students at CSUSM and at the nearby public schools.

With the context of this history in mind, the university founders aimed to create a climate where diversity is valued and celebrated. Consider the university's mission statement:

> CSU San Marcos endorses an international perspective that addresses the global community in its distinctive social, political, and economic terms. This multicultural outlook is reflected in our curriculum, extracurricular activities, international exchanges, and special programs that focus on world issues and problems. (CSUSM, 1994, p. 3)

Yet San Marcos is also near one of the nation's largest military installments, accounting for a conservative majority of voters. Indeed, the conservative political majority in the area is often at odds with minority concerns and the university mission.

The university has grown from 250 full-time students to 3,250 full-time freshman through graduate students in its 8 years of existence. The student body includes 26% who are ethnic minorities. Currently, 35% of university tenure-line faculty are from underrepresented populations. In pursuit of its commitment to diversity, CSUSM has rigorous undergraduate requirements in foreign language and in course work addressing issues of race, class, gender, and global awareness.

The College of Education

The College of Education has been purposeful in its efforts to prepare candidates for multicultural, multilingual teaching contexts. As with the university mission statement, the college mission statement addresses the importance of acting on the belief that *all* students can learn, that teachers are the primary agents for this learning, and that teachers must be lifelong learners skilled at problem solving and collaboration with their peers. In the hiring process, the faculty who have been hired since the adoption of the mission statement (22 of 26 tenured or tenure-line faculty) addressed the ways in which they see themselves promoting the mission of the college. An added result is that faculty of color, drawn to the notion of inclusion and collaboration, compose 30% of the faculty, and 70% of the faculty members are women.

Several programmatic decisions exemplify practices consistent with the mission statement. Candidates are placed in cohorts of 25 where they take all their courses together. This serves to facilitate a sense of being in a community of learners where collaboration skills are valued because they are necessary for working with diverse school populations. Second, the college decided to incorporate into all teacher education programs a new state license—Cross-Cultural, Language, and Academic Development (CLAD)—given to teachers prepared to serve students emerging in English-language proficiency. To meet the requirements for this license, a new course, titled "The Role of Cultural Diversity in Schooling," became an admissions prerequisite. Likewise, certain courses were rewritten to have more credit hours for the express purpose of infusing the competencies associated with the CLAD certificate. Third, bilingual candidates are integrated throughout the cohorts; they receive the Bilingual Crosscultural, Language, and Academic Development license on completion. Thus, the English-only candidates have the opportunity to work with the bilingual candidates (discouraging the segregation between these two faculties evidenced in most schools); this assures that all candidates understand the theories and methods of bilingual education and allows bilingual candidates to influence and educate other candidates in a way only peers can. Last, the college actively recruits and retains students of color interested in pursuing their teaching credentials via its "teacher diversity" efforts. These efforts provide scholarships to students, fund ethnic minority students to take course work geared to helping them meet the requirements for entry into the college, and sponsor a yearly "Teaching as a Career" day, aimed at 150 ethnic minority high school students.

The Middle Level Teacher Education Program

The program we have created to prepare middle level teachers for multicultural, multilingual school settings is a full-time, two-semester, postbaccalaureate program leading to both elementary and middle level teaching licenses (for a complete description of the program, see

McDaniel, Rios, & Stowell, 1995). Attention to issues of diversity begins with the admissions interview when applicants are asked to describe their experiences with, and vision for, meeting the needs of students from culturally and linguistically diverse backgrounds.

Course work is taught on site in a dedicated classroom in a middle school whose student body is culturally and linguistically diverse. Being on site puts us in the thick of things (May, 1992), providing our candidates the opportunity to observe and interact with the culturally and linguistically diverse middle school students and their (less diverse) teachers on a regular basis.

To model what we consider good middle level practice and to provide a coherent teacher education program, the middle level program is taught by six instructors as an interdisciplinary team. The team designs assignments that address multicultural, multilingual goals as much as possible. For example, unit plans are assessed by all instructors for the appropriateness of instruction for ethnic and linguistic minority students. In our course work, we incorporate content of a multicultural nature. Through our team teaching of content that is both multicultural and meaningful, we see ourselves as part of a much-needed teacher education "revolution" to produce "critical thinkers who are multiculturally and globally informed and capable of understanding and addressing the needs of diverse students" (Garcia & Pugh, 1992, p. 219).

In addition to the team-planned and team-taught topics, each team member incorporates competencies from the CLAD license into his or her individual course topics. For example, in the "Teaching and Learning in the Middle School" course, the two instructors teach the candidates to incorporate into all lessons specially designed academic instruction in English (SDAIE, more widely known as *sheltered instruction*). The team members who teach methods course work in mathematics, science, and social studies for middle schools then model those SDAIE approaches and require the candidates to demonstrate competency in using them for that content area. In all of our course work, we model the use of authentic forms of assessment that ask candidates to demonstrate what they know rather than exposing what they do not know.

Last, field experiences are designed to help our candidates make substantial contact with students from culturally and linguistically diverse backgrounds. We strive to place our candidates, during one of their two student teaching experiences, with a teacher holding a license in teaching multilingual students in a multicultural, multilingual settings.

The Course and Course Work

The only course in the middle level program that is entirely devoted to issues of diversity is "Theories and Methods of Bilingual-Multicultural Education." This course is taught over the two semesters of the program and focuses on topics such as defining culture, exploring the relationship between culture and language with its implications for cross-cultural communication, learning how to use ethnographic techniques for learning about others, examining theories of multicultural education and theories of bilingual education (including second-language acquisition), developing specific strategies for multiculturalizing curriculum and instruction as well as techniques for promoting academic success, and understanding the role of English language development for students emerging in their English proficiency.

The first assignment for this course is a "cultural plunge" that requires a group of candidates (3-5) to learn about a cultural group different from their own via a review of the literature and making contact with (or providing community service for) individuals from that community. The second assignment requires candidates to debate or examine an issue of critical importance: Why we should provide access to public education for the children of undocumented workers; Why we need bilingual education, and so on. These topics are "loaded" to result in particular types of responses. In discussing this with the candidates, the instructor contends that no information is politically neutral, that the candidates are more likely to be exposed to the opposite point of view on these topics than they are to the point of view they are asked to take, and that they need only understand, not necessarily agree with, this viewpoint, as in any debate. The instructor is explicit about the ethical dilemma he confronts: the deliberate bias of his teaching against the possibility that candidates' negative biases about these issues persuasively delivered could increase stereotypes, prejudices, and so forth in others.

■ Methods

Participants

The participants of this study were 15 preservice teachers (13 females, 2 males) who were enrolled in the middle level teacher education program and who consented to voluntary participation.[1] Two of the candidates were Chicana; all other participants were European American.

The Survey

A survey was administered to the participants during the first class meeting of "Theories and Methods of Bilingual-Multicultural Education." The survey (see Appendix) asked the participants to define what *multicultural education* means, the implications of that definition (for society, schools, curriculum, etc.), their experiences dealing with people from diverse backgrounds, their degree of comfort communicating about issues of diversity and with people different from themselves, and questions about teaching students from diverse backgrounds.

The participants were asked to anonymously respond as completely as possible to the prompts provided in the survey. When finished, the survey was collected. On completion of the semester's course work and field experiences, the original surveys were placed on a table, and candidates were asked to find their papers. They were instructed to make changes, additions, deletions, and so on to what they had originally written. They were to do this in a way that distinguished these new reflections from the original by using a different colored pencil or pen (supplied by the instructor). On completion, the surveys were collected.

The Coding Scheme

Before analyzing the surveys, two faculty members experienced with and knowledgeable about multicultural education read the participants' responses. Following the principles of grounded theory research (Glaser & Strauss, 1967), indicators relevant to the affect of the candidates with respect to their preparation to work in multicultural-multilingual middle level settings were identified and then refined through repeated examination of the data. A reconciliation of ambiguous or contradictory information and a synthesis of the data were approached. The two noted very little academic change from the precourse to the postcourse survey writing. What emerged from data analysis was that candidates *felt* more strongly about multicultural and multilingual education. The surveys suggested the theoretical construct to apply—in this case, Krathwohl's *Taxonomy* (Krathwohl et al., 1964), which focuses on the affective domain. The two faculty members collaboratively reconstructed the taxonomy to reflect the themes and ideas they saw emerging from the survey data (Figure 10.2 and Table 10.1). In so doing, they described each category in the taxonomy as completely as possible. This

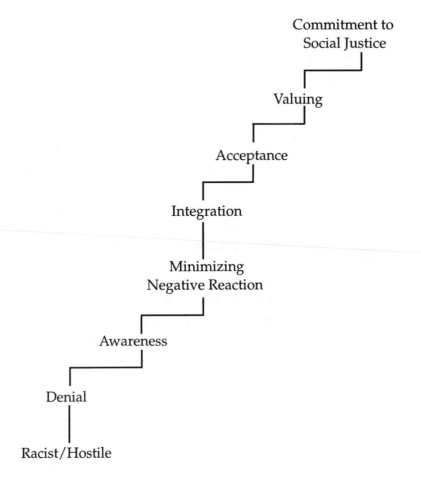

Figure 10.2. Affective Taxonomy for Multicultural Education

reconstructed version of Krathwohl's *Taxonomy* applied to the candidates' experiences is here called the Affective Taxonomy for Multicultural Education.

Once this taxonomy was completed, exemplars (actual examples that typified each category) were selected to illustrate the categories. What was interesting during this search was that natural "bridge" statements were often evident showing how candidates were moving from one category to another in their thinking. It should be noted that although we had asked the candidates to delete statements they no longer believed in, there were no deletions at all.

TABLE 10.1 Descriptive Categories for the Affective Taxonomy of Multicultural Education

1. Racist-Hostile	Statements that are explicitly racist or openly hostile to issues of diversity, multiculturalism, bilingualism, and so on.
2. Denial	Statements that deny or question the need for diversity by suggesting that dealing with diversity is not an issue.
3. Awareness	Statements suggesting multicultural education is about increasing awareness-understanding (via knowledge) of diversity, multiculturalism, and so on.
4. Minimizing Negativity	Statements that focus on minimizing the negative reactions (bias, prejudice, stereotyping, etc.) associated with diversity, bilingualism, and so on.
5. Integration	Statements suggesting that multicultural education is about having people be integrated, get along, work together, and so on.
6. Acceptance-Respect	Statements that suggest that the focus of multicultural education should be the fostering of acceptance and respect for people who are diverse, speak multiple languages, and so on.
7. Valuing	Statements that show a deeper degree of passion (appreciation, championing, etc.) for multiculturalism, bilingualism, diversity, and so on.
8. Commitment to Social Justice	Statements that suggest feeling so strongly about cultural and linguistic diversity that the person is willing to act to promote a more fair, just society.

Next, two teaching team members reanalyzed the data to quantify the number of times student comments appeared for each category during the precourse and postcourse surveys. The two independently counted the number of instances of words, phrases, or whole sentences indicative of each category. They then met to discuss areas of disagreement or omission by one or the other, clarifying the categories and arriving at complete interrater agreement.

TABLE 10.2 Quantitative Results of Changes in Student Thinking About Diversity

Value	Precourse Survey Statements/Respondents	Postcourse 01 Survey Statements/Respondents
Racist-Hostile	0/0	0/0
Denial	0/0	0/0
Awareness	36/14	9/8
Minimizing Negativity	15/8	6/4
Integration	56/15	25/9
Acceptance-Respect	25/9	15/11
Valuing	15/8	21/12
Commitment to Social Justice	13/8	36/12

NOTE: $N = 15$.

■ Results

The Taxonomy

We now describe each category of the taxonomy and present exemplar statements taken from the survey. Where we found them, we also include examples of bridge statements candidates made connecting one category to another. At the end, we provide quantitative data showing the number of candidates making the number of statements both in the precourse and postcourse survey.

Racist-Hostile

As has been described elsewhere (Garcia & Pugh, 1992), we expected that some of the survey respondents might be hostile to the notion of multicultural education and its implications. Therefore, we looked for statements that were explicitly racist or openly hostile to issues of diversity, multiculturalism, bilingualism, and so on. We did not find any of these statements.

Denial

Likewise, Garcia and Pugh (1992) found in their study that some students had denied issues of diversity. Thus, we looked for statements that the respondents made in which they either denied any increase in the diverse composition of our schools and society or suggested that dealing with diversity was unimportant. We did not find any of these statements.

Awareness

We describe this category as the value construct centered around becoming aware of and understanding diversity and all its implications. Thus, we searched for statements that suggested multicultural education is about increasing awareness and understanding (via knowledge) of diversity, multiculturalism, bilingualism, and so on. Consider the following exemplars (the initials indicate individual respondents):

"Striving for cultural awareness—in self and in others" (SS)

"Educating students to the various world cultures" (AA)

"A curriculum which relates to the ethnic and cultural background of the students" (CC)

Of note is the bridge statement provided by TQ:

We need to teach the relationship of the people in one culture to other cultures. If we know more about them we can learn to get along better . . . to coexist with others who have different cultures and values. (TQ)

Minimizing Negative Reactions

In this category, we looked for statements that focused on minimizing negative reactions to diversity, such as bias, prejudice, stereotyping, and so on. We hypothesized that to minimize negativity, one must already be aware (at some level) of diversity. We did find some examples of this kind of statement:

Educate students to put aside their prejudices (KX)

Providing a less ethnocentric learning atmosphere (SS)

[The teacher] putting aside beliefs and prejudices and objectively teaching the lesson. It requires a constant vigilance in recognizing and rooting out the subtle prejudices we all develop toward children. (TI)

> Get away from stereotyping leading to being designated failures or retarded (KX)

What was interesting was the bridge statement describing the limitation of this value construct: "This is a good start, but it's reactive—a more proactive approach would be to present curriculum materials which represent multiple perspectives." (LC)

Getting Along

As LC suggested, the next value level would focus on getting along—the integration of people and curriculum. Thus, we looked for statements that suggested that multicultural education is about having people be integrated, get along, work together, or that the curriculum itself ought to be integrated with multiple points of view. For example,

> Blend cultural differences into a colorful montage (SS)
>
> The ability to live in peace without changing their culture (BG)
>
> Involve viewpoints (in the curriculum) from all ethnic backgrounds (KQ)
>
> Unity (KX)

Acceptance-Respect

We hypothesized, based on the Krathwohl model, that the next value level would be typified by acceptance and respect. We searched for statements suggesting that the focus of multicultural education should be fostering acceptance and respect for people who are diverse, speak multiple languages, and so on. For our exemplars, we identified the following:

> The validation of the multiple cultures in our culture (MB)
>
> Treating each other's culture with respect (CC)
>
> Validating of knowledge, values, and history of a variety of cultures (OT)
>
> Respect and working with differences (KQ)

Of note is the bridge statement between this level and next supplied by LC: "It's not just accepting but valuing." (LC)

Valuing

The next value levels indicate greater passion about diversity. Thus, for this level, we searched for statements that showed a deeper degree of passion (appreciation, championing, etc.) for multiculturalism, bilingualism, diversity, and so on. Consider our exemplars:

Prizing the similarities and differences among one another (MB)

Finding an appreciation for diversity (AA)

Celebrating the rich life experience we gain with diversity (CC)

Show that diversity is valued (KS)

A bridge between this level and the level where one is characterized, as a result of their behavior, by the value complex was written by OT:

It requires major changes in attitudes of society (including teachers) concerning how things should be decided and by whom. Instigating a change in the power base that exists means empowering those who have no voice or minimum effect on the status quo. This could be accomplished by an education system that values and encourages diversity and creative thinking in all students. (OT)

Commitment to Social Justice

As OT suggested, one can become empowered and make major changes toward social justice once the education system values diversity in all its students. We searched for statements made that suggested that the respondents felt so strongly about cultural and linguistic diversity that they were willing to act to promote a more fair, just society. Our exemplars follow:

Claim our (minority) rights for equal access and equal opportunity in this society (MB)

Teaching critical thinking skills about social and ethnic issues . . . address oppression openly. (KX)

Everything has to change: curriculum materials, curriculum content, teacher perspectives, institutional strategies, student evaluation, visuals, home-school relationships, extracurricular activities. (SS)

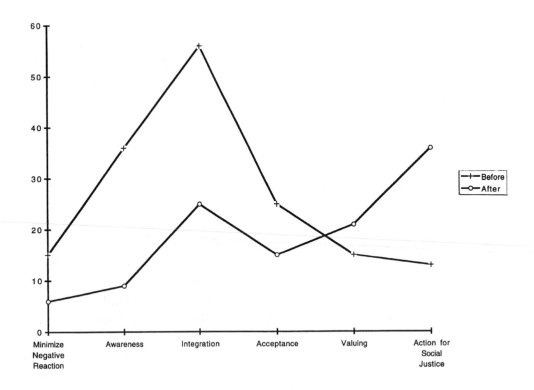

Figure 10.3. Line Chart of Changes in Student Thinking About Diversity

> We must take some responsibility for shaping individuals and take
> some positive actions toward ending oppression . . . [and] em-
> power students and give them a reason to become literate. (KQ)

With respect to the quantitative results, all the candidates showed a
range of affective comments; no respondent seemed stuck at one particular level. Still, as illustrated in Table 10.2 and Figure 10.3, the candidates during the first administration made a majority of statements in
the beginning categories, whereas we see a marked upward trend in the
latter categories during the second administration. As described earlier,
candidates did not delete their original statements between the precourse and postcourse administrations of the survey but simply added
on. HL described this: "My ideas about multicultural education have
been refined, although I haven't changed my original outlook." (HL)

In this regard, Figure 10.4 is a better description of the quantitative
results.

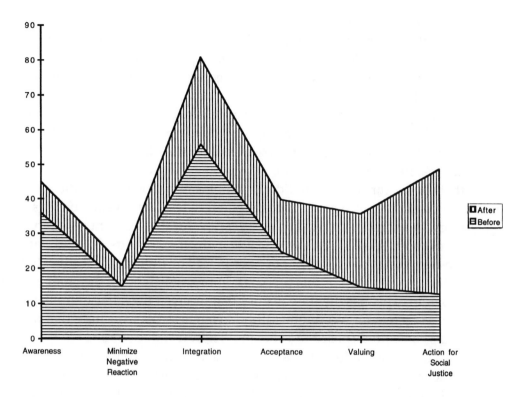

Figure 10.4. Area Chart (Stacked) of Changes in Student Thinking About Diversity

■ Analysis and Discussion

What explains the positive gains in levels of affect regarding issues of diversity? It would be difficult at best to live in Southern California, 60 miles north of the United States-Mexican border, and not have some degree of multicultural awareness or at least give lip service to it. Furthermore, the residents of Southern California who participated in this study attended a university and a college of education in which multicultural issues play a primary role (some suggest they come here because of it). The mission of the university and of the college, the number of ethnic minority faculty members, and courses around issues of diversity all work to bring candidates to the middle level program with an awareness of multiculturalism. Candidates also come to a university and college that are working to increase the diversity of the student population and so the chances of working alongside peers from diverse ethnic and linguistic groups are high.

Perhaps the university serves as a supportive environment in which students can begin to explore multiculturalism. It is (hopefully) a safe place where students can begin to develop some thinking, some attitudes, and even some action regarding equity and social justice. The university then acts as a kind of laboratory or a zone of proximal development (Vygotsky, 1978). Students can rehearse ways that they can act outside of the university setting and develop some strategies to use when they are teachers in diverse classrooms. As teacher educators, we are grateful to our university colleagues for the work done before us so that we can further the candidates' notions of multicultural education.

Candidates also come to be prepared to teach in diverse school settings. In addition, the qualifying interview for the program asks candidates about issues regarding teaching in diverse contexts. So candidates are alerted early on to the importance placed on multicultural education in the program. All of this preparation prior to entering the credential program explains why the category that received the largest number of responses overall was multicultural awareness. We conclude that students come predisposed to value multicultural education.

The transition from the Krathwohl's affective taxonomy to the construction of the Affective Taxonomy for Multicultural Education served to illustrate shifts in candidates' attitudes about multicultural education once they entered the teacher education program. However, the category descriptors were not entirely complete and clean; some concepts proved problematic. For example, some lingering questions exist about which descriptors show more passion (or less) regarding diversity (e.g., where does "minimizing negativity" fit—before or after awareness?). In addition, there appeared to be more happening in the shift from one level to another than the category names described. We hypothesize that perhaps there are half steps or substeps in moving from one category to another. For example, "sensitivity" might be a half step between minimizing negativity and integration. Nonetheless, although these levels of the taxonomy were problematic because they blended one to the next, the candidates' comments about diversity were distinguishable (note our interrater agreement).

We conclude that the candidates grew especially in the latter two areas of the taxonomy. Although there was not much quantitative change, there were some important qualitative additions. Students constructed knowledge and attitudes about diversity layer by layer. They did not acquire new perceptions as much as they built on prior knowledge. Candidates were not willing to release formerly held attitudes and beliefs; they resisted changing the perceptions held prior to their credential program. However, the affect they did develop had the benefit of increasing the likelihood of action. Due to their new knowledge and attitudes, we hypothesize that they will not be satisfied with holding particular beliefs or attitudes; rather, they must do something about those beliefs. Because our results demonstrate growth in the area of social justice, we believe that many candidates have begun to see the moral necessity of wedding attitude to action.

Our results further suggest that the cumulative effect of the synergy of the various components of the program, college, university, and community worked to shift candidates' attitudes and beliefs. Students showed an increase in passion regarding multicultural education. This cannot be attributed to any one level (i.e., community, university, college, program, etc.) or component within that level (teacher, course, etc.). Rather, we assert, all are responsible.

Questions Left Unanswered

What, then, were the factors or combination of factors that were especially salient in producing the resulting change in these candidates? The factors at work were the powerful context of diversity at the university and in the community, the mission of the university and college, the diversity of the faculty, field experiences in diverse school settings, the ethnic and gender diversity of candidates within the program, and the academic content and instruction. The dynamic interaction of these factors was at work. It would be difficult at best, if not impossible, to extrapolate what precisely affected the shift in thinking and attitudes of these candidates. Although it would be valuable for teacher educators to know what precipitates a change in attitude and consequently in action, identifying the multitude of variables along with all possible interactions poses a monumental task that may be insurmountable.

We do wonder to what degree candidates stated what they thought their instructors wanted to hear. This survey was administered in a multicultural education course in a teacher education program that places a high value on multicultural issues. The instructor of the course was Latino as were three candidates in the program. Although the three Latino candidates would not see the results of the survey, the instructor would. Anonymity, we argue, does not guarantee honesty.

We are also led to ask the question, Does a certain level of affect translate into action, beyond naming it? Must a particular level of affect precede action? Is it necessary for candidates to pass through levels of affect to be moved to act? Do particular stances develop before others? For example, is it necessary not only to accept others but to value them before moving to act for social justice? How much affect must develop before an individual feels compelled to act?

In addition, we ask, How long will these changes last? The second administration of the survey occurred 5 weeks after the course ended. We are hopeful the candidates don't simply shed the skins of the teachings of the program at its conclusion. However, we are keenly aware that candidates who are offered teaching positions because of their unique preparation often find that other teachers at the school do not welcome this new perspective and approach to instruction and that many schools do not have materials to support these new approaches nor administrators who know how to evaluate these social justice classrooms. Our graduates will experience the usual problems all new teachers face, but will their difficulties be attributed to new methods and materials rather than their own lack of teaching experience? Although we are confident that many of these novice teachers will succeed, others may accept what they perceive as the reality of the traditional teaching they see around them. Rather than being change agents who can revitalize schools, they may adopt the practices of the teachers with whom they work. Rather than changing the system, will they be changed by it? We hope to follow up on this study to investigate how our graduates have fared, what kinds of support they are receiving that is valuable, and how we might continue to support their efforts.

Implications for Teaching and Teacher Education

This study suggests that teacher educators must begin by examining their own practice. We must translate our own affect into action. How well do our own actions represent our attitudes and beliefs? Do we tolerate multiculturalism, value it, or establish classrooms for *our* students that are just and equitable? Can we be accused of asking candidates to do as we say and not as we do?

This examination must then be extended to the college, university, and community. A teacher education program does not exist in isolation. Here, we suggest that the various components interact to advance student thinking and attitudes along the taxonomy we propose. Therefore, there must be an alliance of the partners in this process to commit to the vision of a just and equitable society.

This study reminds us that teacher preparation is more than knowledge of theory and methods; it is also about developing the affective domain. It serves to reinforce Goodlad's (1990) notion of teaching as a moral endeavor. Attitudes and values will be attained with or without the attention of teacher educators. Therefore, it is equally as critical that we teach, model, and discuss the kinds of attitudes and values that would be most effective and most just in increasingly diverse classrooms. Knowledge without affect will not be acted on, and of what use is knowledge not acted on? The writer George Eliot commented, "Knowledge that is arid, that is not connected in some way to a moral vision, is all too futile and even dangerous." We must be clear about our vision and the values and knowledge that bring that vision to life.

■ Appendix: Multicultural Education Survey

1. What does multicultural education (generally) mean to you? Define multicultural education.
2. What does this definition mean for schools? For society?
3. Discuss the implications this definition has with respect to
   A. Curriculum
   B. Instruction-Teaching
   C. School Policies
   D. Students
4. What experiences have you had working or studying in multicultural environments?
5. What academic experiences have you had in multicultural education (course work, workshops, etc.)?
6. How comfortable (or uncomfortable) do you feel about talking about issues of race, gender, handicap, and sexual orientation? What topics are especially uncomfortable for you? Why?
7. How comfortable do you feel talking with people whose race, gender, handicap, or sexual orientation is different from your own? Which groups are especially uncomfortable for you to communicate with? Why?
8. What special differences have you noted in interacting with people from diverse ethnic or linguistic backgrounds? How did you deal with those differences?
9. What questions do you want addressed in this program with respect to teaching students from diverse *ethnic* backgrounds? From diverse *linguistic* backgrounds?

■ Note

1. All 22 students who were enrolled in the course agreed to participate. However, 7 of the surveys could not be used: 5 because the student did either the prestep or poststep but not both (usually due to absence from class); 2 because the students did not return their surveys at the end of the semester.

■ References

California State University–San Marcos. (1994). *General catalog, 1994-95.* San Marcos, CA: Author.

Chu, H., & Levy, J. (1988). Multicultural skills for bilingual teachers. *NABE Journal, 12*(2), 17-36.

Collier, J. P. (1985). University models for ESL and bilingual teacher training. In National Clearinghouse for Bilingual Education (Ed.), *Issues in English language development.* Rosslyn, VA: Editor.

Darder, A. (1995). Buscando America: The contribution of critical Latino educators to the academic development and empowerment of Latino students in the U.S. In C. Sleeter & P. McLaren (Eds.), *Multicultural education, critical pedagogy, and the politics of difference* (pp. 319-347). Albany: State University of New York Press.

Dwyer, C. (1991). *Language, culture, and writing* (Working paper 13). Berkeley: University of California, Center for the Study of Writing.

Erickson, F. (1987). Transformation and school success: The politics of culture and educational achievement. *Anthropology and Education Quarterly, 18*(4), 335-356.

Garcia, J., & Pugh, S. L. (1992). Multicultural education in teacher preparation programs: A political or an educational concept? *Phi Delta Kappan, 74*(3), 214-219.

Glaser, B. G., & Strauss, A. L. (1967). *The discovery of grounded theory.* Chicago: Aldine.

Goodlad, J. I. (1990). The occupation of teaching in schools. In J. E. Goodlad, R. Soder, & K. A. Sirotnik (Eds.), *The moral dimensions of teaching* (pp. 3-34). San Francisco: Jossey-Bass.

Krathwohl, D. R., Bloom, B. S., & Masia, B. B. (1964). *Taxonomy of educational objectives: Handbook II, The affective domain.* New York: David McKay.

Ladson-Billings, G. (1992). Culturally relevant teaching: The key to making multicultural education work. In C. Grant (Ed.), *Research and multicultural education* (pp. 106-121). London: Falmer.

Locke, D. (1988). Teaching culturally different students: Growing pine trees or bonsai trees? *Contemporary Education, 59*(1), 130-133.

Martin, R., & VanGunten, D. M. (1994, February). *Altering the attitudes of teacher education students regarding issues of diversity: A challenge for transformative pedagogues.* Paper presented at the annual meeting of the National Association of Multicultural Education, Detroit, MI.

May, W. T. (1992). Review of the book *Empowerment through multicultural education. Journal of Teacher Education, 43*(2), 149-152.

McDaniel, J. E., Rios, F. A., & Stowell, L. P. (1995). California State University-San Marcos. In K. McKwin & T. Dickerson (Eds.), *The professional preparation of middle level educators.* Columbus, OH: National Middle School Association.

McDiarmid, G. W. (1992). What to do about differences? *Journal of Teacher Education, 43*(2), 83-93.

McDiarmid, G. W., & Price, J. (1993). Preparing teachers for diversity: A study of student teachers in a multicultural program. In M. J. O'Hair & S. J. Odell (Eds.), *Diversity and teaching: ATE teacher education yearbook 1* (pp. 31-59). Fort Worth, TX: Harcourt Brace Jovanovich.

National Association of State Directors of Teacher Education and Certification. (1984). *NASDTEC certification standards.* Washington, DC: Author.

Pease-Alvarez, L., Espinoza, P., & Garcia, E. (1991). Effective schooling in pre-school settings: A case study of LEP students in early childhood. *Early Childhood Research Quarterly*, pp. 153-164.

Rios, F., & Whitehorse, D. (1994). A passion for multicultural education. In Kappa Delta Pi (Ed.), *Insights on diversity.* West Lafayette, IN: Editor.

Sleeter, C. E. (1992). Restructuring schools for multicultural education. *Journal of Teacher Education, 43*(2), 141-148.

Villegas, A. M. (1991). *Culturally responsive pedagogy for the 1990's and beyond.* Princeton, NJ: Educational Testing Service.

Vygotsky, L. S. (1978). *Mind and society.* Cambridge, MA: Harvard University Press.

Multicultural Education in Practice

What Do Teachers Say?

- *Constance L. Walker*
- *Diane J. Tedick*

■ Putting Theory Into Practice

Everywhere in education, one can find the terms *diversity* and *multicultural education*. Attention to the reality of diverse school populations and the call for a multicultural perspective in our schools have been common themes in recent years. National reform efforts, professional educational organizations, and state educational offices have gone on record as supporting a paradigm shift from a monocultural exclusive curriculum to one that expands itself to consider the reality of U.S. cultural pluralism. Multicultural education is a philosophy that underlies the effort to provide young people with an education that is "equal and excellent" (Nieto, 1996, p. 307). According to Nieto, it is antiracist and antidiscriminatory, basic, pervasive, and important for all students; it is also a process: It involves education for social justice and embodies critical pedagogy; as such, she would argue the need to consider the sociopolitical context of education as we explore alternatives to an educational system that spells failure for a great number of students.

There is much literature outlining the rationale for multicultural education and describing curricular and instructional strategies for attending to issues of race, gender, disability, and social class. In recent years, the voices supporting the theories for a multicultural, gender-fair, disability-aware curriculum have urged that teachers address the reality of diverse student populations and examine the standard curriculum and traditional teaching practices in order that substantial changes be made that reflect that reality (Banks, 1994; Banks & Banks, 1989; Nieto, 1996; Sleeter, 1990, 1991; Sleeter & Grant, 1994; Weis & Fine, 1993). Several texts have addressed the need for teachers to examine actual model lessons that are transformed into those that expand their themes to encompass other cultural and subcultural perspectives (e.g., Grant & Sleeter, 1989). When teachers are questioned as to their own preparedness or their school or district's preparedness to meet the needs of culturally and linguistically different children, they consistently report that although they see a need for preparation in this area, the need is not met (Rashid, 1990). Over the years, our experiences with teachers from a variety of metropolitan, suburban, and rural school districts have supported the fact that at the school district level, the implementation of multicultural education has been assumed without an opportunity for teachers to explore, through collaboration, the ways in which such implementation can best be accomplished. Given the delicate, controversial, and potentially inflammatory nature of discussions about race, ethnicity, language, and sexual orientation in society as a whole, the absence of such opportunity has indeed become part of the problem of considering multicultural education in schools. Not only has there been little attempt to examine the foundation for such profound changes in thought and practice where culture and schooling are concerned, but the complexity of multicultural education—its potential effects on everything from textbooks to teacher behaviors—does not easily lend itself to research. As recently as 1987, Sleeter and Grant found no actual research studies on multicultural education practice in classrooms. They argued that efforts are needed to move beyond advocacy, issues, and courses of action to exploring "what happens when teachers work with multicultural education in their classrooms, what forms it takes and why, how students respond, and what barriers are encountered" (Sleeter & Grant, 1987, p. 438). We would argue that before such studies proliferate, there is first a need to examine the conceptualization with which teachers begin the process of multicultural education and, more important, teachers' perceptions of their own abilities to make change within their own classrooms or within a particular school context. We must recognize that despite clarion calls for multicultural education, teachers and school administrators are fundamentally conservative in their views of diversity. Evans (1991) argues for "the need for in-depth research which develops a clearer understanding of teacher conceptions, practices, and student beliefs vis-à-vis cultural diversity" (p. 12).

We know very little about how teachers approach issues of diversity in their own classrooms or whether the support for change exists within buildings and districts. Given the visible nature of multicultural education across the educational spectrum in the United States, what support exists for teachers to attend to the issues that compose multicultural education? What conflicts exist?

■ Teachers Address the Issues of Multicultural Education

Working with a group of 28 teachers enrolled in a course on multicultural education, we decided to explore these questions. Using participants' written descriptions of the manifestations of diversity in their districts and schools sites, as well as their own plans for implementing multicultural education, we sought to explore concepts of diversity in their schools, the levels of support for implementing change, and their strategies for developing a more multicultural approach to teaching.

Our teacher education programs serve the Twin Cities of Minneapolis and St. Paul, a large metropolitan area of 2.2 million people within Minnesota, a Midwestern state with a total population twice that number. The primary students of color who attend schools in the metropolitan area are African American, Southeast Asian (primarily Hmong, Lao, and Vietnamese), and Hispanic (primarily Mexican American). Only in the actual districts of Minneapolis and St. Paul do students of color compose any significant proportion of the school population: 65% in Minneapolis, and 51% in St. Paul.

The group of teachers consisted of 28 individuals enrolled in a graduate level course at the University of Minnesota, 19 females and 9 males. Twenty-seven of the 28 were currently teaching or preparing to teach. Of these, 20 were European Americans, and 8 described themselves as persons of color (3 African Americans, 1 African, 1 Hmong, 1 Taiwanese, 1 Mexican, and 1 Spaniard). They ranged in age from 21 years to 46 years, with 11 considered novice teachers (six years or less in the classroom, including those who were preparing to teach) and 15 veterans (more than six years of teaching). Four were elementary teachers, 3 were currently teaching at the postsecondary level, and 21 were secondary teachers (10, second languages; 4, English; 2, music; 4, social studies; and 1 reading specialist.) Of the group currently teaching, 3 were in urban classrooms and 17 in suburban classrooms.

The course, which we team taught, was an introduction to issues related to multicultural, gender-fair education. The purpose of the course was to explore both the issues underlying multicultural education and some options for considering change as a teacher. The course relied on multiple viewpoints, and we included as guest participants several individuals whose lives and work reflected diverse perspectives (e.g., American Indian values, Afro-centric schools, the gay and lesbian community, etc.). Integral components of the course were presentations from teachers who were teaching within a multicultural framework and an opportunity for participants to experience, read, reflect, converse, and develop lessons and activities for their own teaching settings. To elicit participants' conceptions of how issues of diversity are manifested in their districts or school settings, we asked them to respond in writing to the following prompt:

> Reflecting on your own instructional setting, write informally about the way in which diversity is manifested, reflected, and attended to in your school district and in your school building itself. What are the most visible or tangible elements of diversity? What choices have been made, what level of involvement have teachers and students had in that process, and what has been the atmosphere?

At the end of the course, we were interested in exploring the kinds of actions the course participants were planning to take to implement the principles of multicultural education. They were asked to develop an "action plan" for making small, steady, and meaningful changes in both their professional and personal lives. In their action plans, teachers were asked to consider what they were currently doing personally or professionally, what changes could be made in the immediate future, and what their plans were for the long term in addressing multicultural education.

As we discuss the responses of teachers, it is important to note the rarefied nature of our sample. All course participants in the group had chosen to enroll in a course on multicultural, gender-fair curriculum. Whether from slight curiosity or strong affinity for the issue, these teachers had made a choice to explore over a 10-week period a topic of great timeliness, interest, and frustration to educators. We do not imagine that this group is representative of all teachers. Yet we found the opportunity to examine the beliefs, perspectives, and potential action of teachers already interested in multicultural education to be of value. Based on their written responses to our prompts, it was clear that they had observed the winds of multicultural education in their own school districts and had considered the ways in which their colleagues were reacting to discussions of the topic; state and district mandates related to a multicultural, gender-fair, disability-aware curriculum; and ways in which teachers might address and respond to diversity in teaching.

■ Multicultural Education in Schools: Complex, Controversial, and Minimally Supported

As we examined the course participants' written descriptions of manifestations of diversity in their schools and districts, we discovered that a primary theme that emerged was the overwhelming nature of multicultural education. Both conceptualizing it and putting it into practice were unanimously viewed as complex, difficult, and requiring of support on a number of levels. Teachers in our group often described the difficulty of thinking about multicultural education as having to do with a lack of a clear understanding of what multicultural, gender-fair curriculum really means. Speaking of both school districts and teachers as individuals, they described this seemingly murky issue as one that invites cynicism and spawns other, more complex difficulties. Without clear agreement on what the term means, teachers in this sample group believed that very few teachers or administrators are prepared to take on the process of exploring what is entailed in rethinking the status quo, examining curricula, and exploring diversity in productive ways.

In late 1988, the state of Minnesota Board of Education adopted a Multicultural and Gender-Fair Disability Aware Curriculum Rule requiring that school boards in each district ensure that a written plan for an inclusive educational program be developed and implemented at the classroom level. In the face of this state mandate to implement multicultural education, school districts have exhibited responses ranging from benign neglect to active implementation. In our work as inservice teacher educators, we have found very few districts on either extreme of the spectrum. Most put forth some efforts at addressing the state guidelines, whether they were token attempts to address diversity or genuine efforts at incorporating multicultural units and lessons into an existing curriculum. We are familiar with only one school (Kindergarten through eighth grade) in the Twin Cities metropolitan area that has systematically used multicultural education as an organizing principle around which the entire curriculum as well as teacher practice is examined. This school is designated specifically as a "multicultural school," receiving special attention and funding from the school district for its efforts, yet each year it must plead for continued support from the administration. More commonly, multicultural education has been filed in the same queue along with other state mandates concerning curriculum and assessment. Several teachers mentioned the superficial and perfunctory nature of their districts' efforts, with districts viewing diversity as a "problem" to be tackled: "We see diversity" as 'others being different than us' rather than a means for growth, empowerment, and opportunity for all." Responding in traditional ways to "new" influences or innovations where multicultural education is concerned, districts might adopt "missions" or year-long school themes that deal with celebrating diversity. Diversity receives a surface treatment through adoption of a slogan, a motto, a committee, or a combination of these. Symbols, buttons, and posters may be evident, but teachers report few changes in actual practice:

> [In our school system,] we acknowledge Black History Month with a poster in the foyer. We invite the African American students to the cafeteria for a muffin. . . . Our district purports that ours is a multicultural, gender-fair curriculum. One needs only to scratch the surface to find out that isn't really true. . . . Often we "talk the good talk" to our students about equality, but the students are savvy enough to recognize that our practices don't always match our words.

Another veteran teacher, active in her suburban district, reports,

> The response to multicultural education is a policy on paper, as far as I can judge. The results have been haphazard and superficial, most left up to the whim of individual schools and faculty members. A public statement of intent does not guarantee the actuality of effective and planned change, but it is good for public relations and may ward off a lawsuit.

A veteran elementary instructor in the same district views the politics of multicultural education in much the same way:

> In terms of having a significant impact on what occurs in classrooms, very little has been achieved, and teachers discern no appreciable

support for multicultural education. Feeble gestures have been made at district workshops and inservices, but they appear [to be] perfunctory exercises.

An interesting perspective was offered by a class member who was a preservice teacher in a postbaccalaureate teacher development program. She described her practicum experience at a suburban junior high school and noted, "I was appalled by the administration's, faculty's, and students' apathy, ignorance, and outright retreat from approaching issues of diversity in the school."

Many teachers in this sample questioned the "top-down" implementation of multicultural, gender-fair curriculum, from its initial mandate at the state level to its trickling down to the school level, with little input from teachers and even less consultation on how it might best fit into classrooms. Even years after districts have developed their own guidelines for multicultural education, staff development has been ignored or superficial, and the role of teachers as the primary implements of change in the classroom has been neglected. Why has this been the case? Teachers reported a prevalent belief that any serious attention to cultural pluralism through adjustment to curriculum or manner of teaching is just another trend. One second-language teacher reported of her suburban school setting, "The atmosphere that I have sensed within the school building about 'multicultural, gender-fair' is, in part, that 'this too, shall pass,' joining as it does Madeline Hunter, modular scheduling, and OBE [Outcome-Based Education]." Another noted his own initial views toward the issue: "My first impression of multicultural education was that of so many other things that happen in education—it is just another fad, and if I can wait it out, I won't have to do much with it."

The history of public education is replete with waves of innovations that were imposed both from within and outside of the educational sector. That multicultural education should be viewed in this light speaks to the experiences of teachers (and communities) with the presentation, rationale, and "packaging" of efforts to impose change on schools. In such a climate, multicultural education has been dismissed by many as just such another passing phase.

A number of teachers in the group mentioned the attention their districts gave to multicultural education by citing the "add on" nature of curricular innovations and teaching strategies suggested for implementation. A Spanish teacher (in a suburban district) in the group was frustrated at her school's efforts, because she believes she already infuses issues related to culture into her teaching:

> We have talked about [this] as a staff and have talked about it like it is something to add, not to incorporate into what you already have. We even get a form to fill out where we need to list our multicultural units so that we look like we're trying to be multicultural.

Rather than being integrated throughout the curriculum, multicultural education is seen as simply the addition of particular lessons or units that reflect an ethnic group, gender differences, or cultural differences. Such an approach posits multicultural education as an "appendage" to the existing curriculum—in the form of special classes, advanced placement courses, electives that comprise special programs. One teacher in a suburban district outlined the nature of such a special program and found it an illuminating illustration of some of the difficult issues inherent in getting to the deeper levels of change.

> I think the program that has had the biggest impact on both high schools in the district concerning multicultural education was the addition of the College in the Schools program from the University. . . . A number of English teachers from the high schools applied for the program. In the application process, we realized that our core curriculum in literature was the 'Canon' of DOWGs—Dead Old White Guys. As a result . . . [we] organized the after-school literature program for teachers to read and discuss "multicultural" literature. . . . From those classes, we challenged ourselves to expand the base that we had been using. We were allocated money to buy new literature textbooks after those classes. As a result, we knew we were looking for books that were multiculturally based. Most of us were excited about that opportunity. Yet one of my colleagues thought the existing "World Literature" text was multicultural because it included an author from France.

Collaboration and cross-disciplinary efforts are increasing in schools as the value of combined efforts is recognized. Yet where multicultural education is concerned, respondents in our sample believed that, in general, teachers are left to address multicultural education in their own ways. It is clear that when left to individual teachers to implement, on the one hand, there is hope that changes within a multicultural framework will be meaningful and lasting; on the other hand, there is tremendous variability in the degree to which individual teachers understand the issues and choose to make changes. As one suburban high school English teacher put it, "Well, we are a diverse school district and high school. Some of this diversity is celebrated with pins and posters and some is lived every day in the 'trenches' causing confusion, pain, growth, and joy." Teachers in the group reported all methods of activity related to multicultural education, from resistance to tempered enthusiasm. One teacher, a veteran African American male urban middle school teacher, described the apathy on the part of staff:

> I think many older teachers do not want to be bothered by all this fuss over diversity and cultural awareness. Most of them live far from the inner city and have little contact with the population they instruct. As is the case with the rest of our society, when no choice is made, you, in effect, are making a choice.

Teachers in the course described various activities taking place at the district or school level, but an interesting theme of isolation emerged in their writing: No matter the state or district mandates for change or the school's movement toward multicultural education, teachers feel that they are on their own. Teachers in the group did not expect detailed blueprints for curricular and course changes to be handed down from district administrators. But, we suspect, neither did they expect that the great burden of exploring issues of diversity would be left to teacher will and initiative. Their writings communicate a level of frustration with both the lack of clarity on the part of larger school entities as well as the lack of administrative commitment and energy to support meaningful change. Most important, they stressed the need for time and the opportunity to examine and discuss these issues with colleagues so that a climate of collaboration and mutual goals could be established. A study of staff development for multicultural education found similar levels of frustration, even among those wanting to consider change in their teaching and decried "the lack of time and opportunity available to learn to think and act differently" (Sleeth, 1990).

■ Teachers' Individual Plans for Addressing Diversity Through Multicultural Education

Researchers who have explored teacher development in the area of multicultural education agree that movement toward a multicultural perspective begins with individual knowledge and awareness (Gay, 1977; Grant & Melnick, 1978; Sleeter, 1992). They argue that in considering professional development in this area, earlier sessions need to explore knowledge and awareness, with later ones stressing teaching skills. Such continua, from the acquisition of knowledge and awareness through to implementation, appear often in the discussions of teacher preparation (Banks, 1994; Banks & Banks, 1989; Cushner, McClelland, & Safford, 1996; Grant & Sleeter, 1989). Burstein and Cabello (1989) include *reflection* as the final step, arguing that teachers need the opportunity to consider their practice where diversity is concerned and to share their experiences and efforts with colleagues. Each of the steps reinforces one another, such that implementing a particular aspect of a curricular unit can help awareness, and seeking knowledge about gender issues or linguistic groups can raise one's awareness of issues related to other aspects of multiculturalism. Sleeter (1992) believes that teachers must first become aware of the basic issues that support a need for multicultural education. She presents four primary categories of the needs that teachers have to become effective at multicultural education: "Teachers must develop a knowledge base about cultural diversity, acceptance of cultural differences and a commitment to serve cultural minority communities, and skills for translating multicultural education into action in the classroom" (p. 33).

Teachers in this study were already predisposed to consider issues of diversity and education, having decided to enroll in an actual course on multicultural education. Exposure to both theory and practice related to multicultural, gender-fair, disability-aware curriculum was accomplished through the quarter-long course itself. The action plan, due at the close of the course, allowed for us to examine where these teachers might go from there. What was the nature of their plans? How extensive would their efforts be to put into practice what they had learned? It came as no surprise that when asked to consider avenues for change in their own professional lives, these teachers began with themselves. In every case, respondents spoke of particular aspects of the course that had affected them personally, emphasizing the need to continue that process of reading, conversation, reflection, and action. Teachers' plans for change fell into three primary categories—self, the classroom setting, and the district or school setting. Virtually all of the teachers began their action plans with discussion about how they individually needed to expand their knowledge and awareness to learn more about other cultures and communities represented both in the United States and the world through reading and interacting with diverse cultures. In addition, they spoke of the need to get to know themselves, to confront their own racism, sexism, or homophobia, and to understand the context in which those attitudes were created as they learned to be more tolerant and understanding. One teacher indicated,

I am trying to strengthen my knowledge as it concerns multicultural, gender-fair issues. The first thing I have done and am still doing is learning more about myself. A reflection of my own culture and gender is helping me to become a more sensitive and much more aware person.

Self-reflection was also a common theme with respect to teachers' plans for changes within their own classrooms. Exploring and reflecting on their own teaching and their relationship with students emerged as an important goal. One teacher questioned his behaviors:

Do I have an agenda that excludes students by race? I feel that sometimes I tend to look out after the African American students a little more. . . . Is my teaching style not sensitive to gender differences? Am I sending messages, being a male, that turn some female students off? . . . These are issues I have no answer for at this time, but I have begun the process of self-examination.

The teachers indicated a desire to critique and reflect on their own behaviors and beliefs, to be aware of whether they are communicating hidden stereotypes, prejudices, or agendas. They also indicated a commitment to interrupting sexist, racist, and homophobic language and behavior and helping students to understand the sources of such language and behavior. One teacher explained that his approach involved telling his students,

I am a racist and a sexist. . . . I further explain to them that since our society is a racist, sexist society, and since I am a product of that society, I am a racist and a sexist. I explain that I am working to become aware of how those things affect me. I am trying to learn about those things so that I don't unconsciously let them affect how I do things.

Other classroom changes discussed by the teachers involve incorporating more cooperative learning activities, creating more student-centered curriculum, and involving students in decision making: "I tend to take for granted what I teach is what [my students] need to know. I feel we must always question ourselves and understand what reality is for ourselves and our students."

Teachers also shared their understanding of the importance of being more critical of texts and materials, creating environments to affirm diversity, and having high expectations for all students. At the larger curricular level, several teachers noted the need to help students to understand themselves in relationship to others. A Spaniard, who is a second-language teacher in an affluent suburb, has made a commitment to have

> a service relationship with a shelter for battered women and their children in which we develop teams of teens that will be creating and implementing programs during the school year. I would like to see them getting involved and planning the activities. This shelter gives my students the opportunity to graduate from the shelter they have been in for many years.

It is clear that although many teachers clearly recognize the need for and importance of systemic change, they feel powerless to influence change beyond their classroom level. As one high school teacher stated,

> The first part of any action plan must . . . be the recognition of the systemic problems in our educational institutions. It has become clear to me that our traditional European curriculum and our social policies reinforce the existing power structures. . . . I must work to change the system rather than "blame the victim." Although I will certainly support changes that the district might make toward a multicultural, gender-fair curriculum, I don't anticipate substantial movement in that direction any time soon, nor would I envision myself leading that crusade. . . . Frankly, I don't have the courage . . . to work to enact school or district-wide changes. Therefore, when I say I must work to change the system, I realize that most of the significant changes will occur in my own classroom.

A teacher's willingness to think differently about the kind of curriculum and instruction she or he coordinates does not ensure that strides toward a multicultural curriculum will be achieved. One committed veteran teacher pointed to the magnitude of accomplishing goals in multicultural education particularly at the school or district level:

> District changes are naturally large scale, cumbersome, and difficult to effect. . . . On a school front, we should continue to push for genuine multicultural education at least in our buildings. I do not believe we can change everything at once, nor should we, necessarily, if we are to do it well. I see it as an ongoing process in which the faculty

needs to be educated as well as the student body. . . . We will need time for ideas to be introduced, explored, accepted or rejected, developed, and finally implemented.

Clearly, from the information given to us by these committed teachers, they struggle with what has to be done. They recognize the tough task of rethinking the relationship between diversity and their teaching and understand that the challenge is immense. From all indications, these teachers, enrolled in a course on multicultural education, understand all too well that one course will not a multicultural teacher make. They describe the complexity of thinking differently about issues of culture and believe that creating major change in the classroom is a long-term and deeply felt personal commitment. In essence, it is a change in self and in the beliefs and theories that underlie practice.

■ The Complex Task of Considering Culture and Diversity in Education

The 28 teachers in our group wanted to make change in their teaching lives where issues of diversity were concerned. Yet many explored in great detail in their action plans the societal, community, school, and professional barriers to effecting changes beyond themselves and their classrooms. The barriers to such change are formidable. Even in urban schools where the minority student population has risen substantially, a serious commitment to major change in school climate and curriculum is not always evident. Even when particular courses begin to include material, resources, or perspectives from other cultures, rarely are students asked to reflect on their own culture in ways that illuminate the common human experience.

Teacher change is only part of the equation. Asking teachers to explore their own feelings and potential for change in what they do is a beginning. This study asked teachers what they saw as the avenues for change in themselves, their schools and districts, and what directions they can take as individuals as well as collectively to work toward such change. Yet teachers in this study understood full well the contextual nature of their teaching, the difficulty in making change in their classrooms that would be supported at home, among students, among faculty peers, the administration, the community, and society at large. Sleeter (1992) reported the same in her comprehensive study of staff development for multicultural education. Many teachers in our study spoke of the difficulty of exploring issues of multicultural education in a climate of backlash for perceived "political correctness" and cited lack of support of the community, administrative staff, and their colleagues for any meaningful changes. Their voices are clear on the matter of risk taking: In an era of fear concerning presentation and exploration of controversial issues, taking risks is often not applauded, encouraged, or modeled.

Multicultural education requires taking risks and getting in the face of controversy. Those teachers who are trying to make changes are doing so within a context of phenomenal conflict: parents and teachers who are vehemently opposed, administrators who may not support their efforts or offer only limited staff development opportunities, and colleagues who believe quite differently about the need to explore and include issues of race, gender, disability, sexual orientation, religion, or social class in the classroom. Clearly, we must recognize that the presence of such a conflictual atmosphere is the direct result of the tension and ambiguity with which the larger society has dealt with issues of diversity. Such conflicts cannot be resolved at the school level while remaining so visibly felt within society as a whole.

Significant change will require time for teachers to meet, to talk, and to create change that will result in meaningful and purposeful experiences for students, opportunities to explore and discuss the very conflicts that confound their society. More recent writings in the field of multicultural education recognize the complexity and depth of the personal, institutional, and social changes necessary for schools to become multicultural environments (Nieto, 1996; Ramsey, 1988; Sleeter, 1992, 1996; Sleeter & McLaren, 1995). Teachers in our study spoke of this complexity as well, and many, in describing the overwhelming nature of multicultural education, realized that it requires a paradigm shift—one that cannot occur in schools or teachers alone but must be mirrored in society.

■ References

Banks, J. A. (1994). *Multiethnic education: Theory and practice* (3rd ed.). Boston: Allyn & Bacon.

Banks, J. A., & Banks, C. A. M. (1989). *Multicultural education: Issues and perspectives.* Boston: Allyn & Bacon.

Burstein, N., & Cabello, B. (1989, September-October). Preparing teachers to work with culturally diverse students: A teacher education model. *Journal of Teacher Education, 40,* 9-16.

Cushner, K., McClelland, A., & Safford, P. (1996). *Human diversity in education. An integrative approach* (2nd ed.). New York: McGraw-Hill.

Evans, R. W. (1991, April). *Educational ideologies and multicultural education.* Paper presented at the Annual Meeting of the American Educational Research Association, Chicago, IL.

Gay, G. (1977). Curriculum for multicultural teacher education. In F. J. Klassen & D. M. Gollnick (Eds.), *Pluralism and the American teacher: Issues and case studies* (pp. 31-62). Washington, DC: American Association of Colleges for Teacher Education.

Grant, C. A., & Melnick, S. L. (1978). Multicultural perspectives of curriculum development and their relationship to in-service education. In R. A. Edelfelt & E. B. Smith (Eds.), *Breakaway to multi-dimensional approaches: Integrating curriculum development and in-service education* (pp. 81-100). Washington, DC: Association of Teacher Educators.

Grant, C. A., & Sleeter, C. E. (1989). *Turning on learning: Five approaches for multicultural teaching.* Columbus, OH: Merrill.

Nieto, S. (1996). *Affirming diversity: The sociopolitical context of multicultural education* (2nd ed.). New York: Longman.

Ramsey, P. G. (1988). *Multicultural teacher education and staff development.* Paper presented at Annual Meetings, American Educational Research Association, New Orleans, LA.

Rashid, H. M. (1990). Teacher perceptions' of the multicultural orientation of their preservice education and current occupation settings. *Educational Research Quarterly, 14*(1), 2-5.

Sleeter, C. E. (1990). Staff development for desegregated schooling. *Phi Delta Kappan, 72*(1), 33-40.

Sleeter, C. E. (1991). *Empowerment through multicultural education.* Albany: State University of New York Press.

Sleeter, C. E. (1992). *Keepers of the American dream: A study of staff development and multicultural education.* London: Falmer.

Sleeter, C. E. (1996). *Multicultural education as social activism.* Albany: State University of New York Press.

Sleeter, C. E., & Grant, C. A. (1987). An analysis of multicultural education in the United States. *Harvard Educational Review, 57*(4), 421-444.

Sleeter, C. E., & Grant, C. A. (1994). *Making choices for multicultural education: Five approaches to race, class, and gender* (2nd ed.). New York: Macmillan.

Sleeter, C. E., & McLaren, P. L. (Eds.). (1995). *Multicultural education, critical pedagogy, and the politics of difference.* Albany: State University of New York Press.

Weis, L., & Fine, M. (Eds.). (1993). *Beyond silenced voices: Class, race, and gender in United States schools.* Albany: State University of New York Press.

12

Old Messages With New Meanings

■ *Mary E. Dilworth*

The research provides numerous instances where teachers' understanding of the background and culture of students precipitates a greater level of learning than is acquired under culturally insensitive conditions (Chavez-Chavez, 1996; Cochran-Smith, 1996; Irvine, 1992). As Darling-Hammond, Dilworth, and Bullmaster (1997) report,

> a growing body of recent work in this area suggests that effective teachers of students of color form and maintain connections with their students within their social contexts. For example, they do not shy away from issues of race and culture; they emphasize issues of content, and substance is given priority over what language is used; they are familiar with the common vernacular even though they instruct in standard English; and they celebrate their students as individuals and as members of specific cultures. . . . There is a significant level of cultural synchronization between teachers and students. (p. 4)

In many ways, the work and reports of the authors in this volume confirm these notions and at the same time, offer some level of optimism in how we can orchestrate learning conditions that promote these critical skills and abilities.

For instance, the parochialism of preservice teachers and the tenacity of educators' preexisting attitudes and beliefs are recognized as conditions that inhibit a teacher's ability to know and understand students from cultures other than their own. Zimpher and Ashburn's (1992) portrayal of those pursuing a teaching career is consistent with the students presented by the authors here: she is

> typically a white female from a small town or suburban community who matriculates in a college less than 100 miles away from home and intends to return to small town America to teach middle-income children of average intelligence in traditionally organized schools. (p. 41)

Also consider that these prospective teachers also exhibit reluctance to teach students from cultures other than their own as well as students who are mentally and physically challenged (American Association of Colleges for Teacher Education, 1989).

The chapters in this volume corroborate these premises over and over again. Virtually all authors speak to the rigidity of neophyte teachers' beliefs and attitudes: the inability or difficulty in unpacking prior understandings, conceptualizing new paradigms, and trusting that there is merit in diversity. Although these insights are familiar to us in prior research, this volume offers a broader variation on the same theme. The fact that these fixed notions appear universal among students as well as seasoned practitioners and are not restricted by age, race-ethnicity, language, or regionality provides a broader dimension to the research that thrives on the limitations of young white preservice students and omits significant attention to the perspectives of others (Dilworth, 1990; Ladson-Billings, 1994).

Consider the similarity in Jane Agee's story of LaTasha, a neophyte African American teacher from the deep South, as she is challenged by her own middle-class background, first in a majority white and subsequently in a diverse school setting, with that of the mostly white teachers that Francisco Rios portrays in the Midwest. Listen to the voice of the young Latina woman, as offered by Reyes, Capella-Santana, and Khisty, who challenged her male relatives in their comfort with stereotypical roles and of Rosenberg's students in the northeast who grapple for meaning in various situations that are only evident to them in a form of entertainment in the movies or on television.

Rosenberg, Webb, and Walker each suggest that the challenge of being culturally responsive also extends to the teachers of teachers—

faculty members in the academy and cooperating teachers in the schools. They posit that all educators ought to be prepared to reexamine their own knowledge base for teaching and be prepared to share their own perspectives on human diversity. The consensus in this volume indicates that no one is exempt from continuing to explore their beliefs and labor for greater understanding of that which is different.

The current trend toward more and authentic assessments of teacher skills and knowledge will presumably help nurture professional development in this area. School systems, teachers, and schools, colleges, and departments of education that train educators are compelled by numerous standard-setting bodies to be more responsive and effective with all students generally and with historically underserved populations specifically. The moral challenges are clear in meeting the expectations of organizations such as National Council on Accreditation of Teacher Education, the Interstate New Teacher Assessment and Support Consortia, the National Board for Professional Teaching Standards, and a host of other state authorities and professional discipline groups. Voids in teacher training and competence relative to diversity are becoming increasingly visible through these new efforts. How "effectiveness" and "competence" will be gauged and the consequences of failure remain to be seen.

The authors in this volume also provide constructive lessons in a number of other education reform areas. We find new insights regarding professional development, assessment, comprehensive and interprofessional practice, and program design.

For example, the transition from the very distinct training components of preservice, inservice, and continuing education to the more coherent and transitional concept of professional development has emerged as one of the most affecting reforms of this decade and has influenced the design and delivery of teaching and teacher education (Dilworth & Imig, 1995; Little, 1993; National Commission on Teaching and America's Future, 1996). In keeping, the notion that teachers are responsible professionals of their own practice and are fully capable of not only acquiring knowledge but of crafting a repertoire of skills that are effective for their students is supported by several of the authors in this volume (for example, see Vavrus and Ozcan, Chapter 6). At the same time, the reality that many aspiring and established teachers are curtailed not only by time, resources, and system restraints but also by limited exposure to cultures other than their own is also in evidence (for example, see Pang & Sablan, Chapter 3). As Darling-Hammond et al. (1996) note, "the extent to which teacher candidates are culturally insular may be a function of limited access to diversity and little tolerance toward difference" (p. 44). It appears that this condition can only be stemmed by comprehensive programs, such as those described by Reyes, Capella-Santana, and Khisty (Chapter 7); Ligons, Rosado, and Houston (Chapter 8), Guillaume, Zuniga, and Yee (Chapter 9); Rios, McDaniel, and Stowell (Chapter 10); and Walker and Tedick (Chapter 11). Through these authors' work, we understand that it is simply not a matter of providing an opportunity to learn but also the quality of knowledge that is offered. This premise helps justify recommendations from reports such as *What Matters Most: Teaching for America's Future* (National Commission on Teaching and America's Future, 1996) for interconnected teacher and teacher education program licensing and certification standards and assessments that have a clear and accurate conception of cultural responsive teaching.

The relationships between and among prospective and established educators also emerges throughout this volume. The findings of Agee, Vavrus and Ozcan, and Pang and Sablan contribute to the belief that cooperating teachers as mentors exhibit a significant amount of influence on their proteges but that this influence is often not well-grounded in the types of knowledge and skills that researchers and scholars of multicultural education hope to propagate. These reports also indicate that more attention ought to be given to those with whom youngsters of any background are reliant for education and learning. As Walker provides, there is a disconnection between the theory of the college and university and the day-to-day challenges and dictates of a pre-kindergarten to 12th grade classroom. There has been substantial rhetoric and work on advancing the concept of school college collaboration especially as it relates to standards setting; little has been done to construct meaningful engagements between practicing teachers and college-based faculty. The new trend toward professional development schools holds promise in this domain, but it is only one format among many.

Last, Michael-Bandele significantly contributes to the notion of the classroom beyond the school and the need for knowledge and services that heretofore have not been considered standard knowledge for classroom teachers. Most important, she translates for us the popular theme, "it takes a village to raise a child," from its natural inception into current-day educational approaches, such as full-service schools as provided by Dryfoos (1994), comprehensive services (Levin, 1994), and the concept of caring for those other than ourselves (Noddings, 1995). She also offers justification for learning in cohort as an effective means for learning about and understanding diversity. This complements and expands the educational reform theme of "learning communities" that are best seen in professional development schools that have increased in number throughout this decade but seldom embrace interprofessional knowledge and practice. The design of teacher education as one that happens in places other than in the academy is also one that is useful to look at from the perspective of human diversity. The opportunity for prospective teachers to learn in schools and communities that are atypical to their experience appears to have merit.

There are numerous messages in this volume for teachers and teacher educators. It is the responsibility of all educators to examine them with a critical eye and glean new meaning from these offerings.

■ References

American Association of Colleges for Teacher Education. (1989). *Teaching teachers facts and figure: RATE III.* Washington, DC: Author.

Chavez-Chavez, R. (1996). *Multicultural education in the everyday: A renaissance for the recommitted.* Washington, DC: American Association of Colleges for Teacher Education.

Cochran-Smith, M. (1995, Winter). Uncertain allies: Understanding the boundaries of race and teaching. *Harvard Educational Review, 65*(4), 541-570.

Darling-Hammond, L., Dilworth, M., & Bullmaster, M. (1997). *Educators of color: The recruitmant, preparation, and retention of persons of color in the teaching profession.* Washington, DC: U.S. Department of Education, Office of Educational Research and Improvement.

Dilworth, M. (1990). *Reading between the lines: Teachers and their racial ethnic cultures.* Washington, DC : ERIC Clearinghouse on Teaching and Teacher Education/American Association of Colleges for Teacher Education.

Dilworth, M., & Imig, D. (1995, Winter). Professional teacher development. *ERIC Review, 3*(3), 5-11.

Dryfoos, J. G. (1994). *Full service schools: A revolution in health and social services for children, youth and families.* San Francisco: Jossey-Bass.

Garcia, E. E. (1993). Language, culture, and education. In L. Darling-Hammond (Ed.), *Review of research in education,* (Vol. 19, pp. 51-98). Washington, DC: American Educational Research Association.

Irvine, J. J. (1992). Making teacher education culturally responsive. In M. Dilworth (Ed.), *Diversity in teacher education: New expectations* (pp. 79-92). San Francisco: Jossey-Bass.

Ladson-Billings, G. (1994). *Dreamkeepers: Successful teachers of African American children.* San Francisco: Jossey-Bass.

Levin, R. (Ed). (1994). *Greater than the sum: Professionals in a comprehensive services model.* Washington, DC: ERIC Clearinghouse on Teaching and Teacher Education.

Little, J. (1993). Teachers' professional development in a climate of educational reform. *Educational Evaluation and Policy Analysis, 15*(2), 129-151.

National Commission on Teaching and America's Future. (1996). *What matters most: Teaching and America's future.* New York: Author.

Noddings, N. (1995). A morally defensible mission for schools in the 21st century. *Phi Delta Kappan, 76*(5), 365-368.

Zimpher, N., & Ashburn, E. (1992). Countering parochialism in teacher candidates. In M. E. Dilworth (Ed.), *Diversity in teacher education: New expectations* (pp. 40-62). San Francisco: Jossey-Bass.

Index

CORWIN
PRESS

The Corwin Press logo—a raven striding across an open book— represents the happy union of courage and learning. We are a professional-level publisher of books and journals for K–12 educators, and we are committed to creating and providing resources that embody these qualities. Corwin's motto is "Success for All Learners."